W9-ATF-357

THREE MODERN SATIRISTS:
WAUGH, ORWELL, AND HUXLEY

THREE MODERN SATIRISTS:

WAUGH, ORWELL,

AND HUXLEY

by Stephen Jay Greenblatt

New Haven and London, Yale University Press

Copyright © 1965 by Yale University.
Fifth printing, November 1968.
Designed by Sally Sullivan,
set in Baskerville type,
and printed in the United States of America by
The Carl Purington Rollins Printing-Office
of the Yale University Press.
All rights reserved. This book may not be
reproduced, in whole or in part, in any form
(except by reviewers for the public press),
without written permission from the publishers.

Library of Congress catalog card number: 65–11180

Distributed in Great Britain, Europe, Asia, and
Africa by Yale University Press Ltd., London; in
Canada by McGill University Press, Montreal; and
in Latin America by Centro Interamericano de Libros
Académicos, Mexico City.

YALE COLLEGE SERIES

The tradition of undergraduate writing and publishing has long been a very lively one at Yale, as witnessed by the large number of periodicals, journalistic or literary in character, which have appeared on the Yale campus. These, however, fail to give an accurate picture of the high proportion of good and original scholarly writing which is also done by undergraduates. The excellence of many of the Honors theses written by Yale Seniors made it desirable some years ago to give the most deserving of them the circulation which publication in printed form could provide. Between 1941 and 1957 ten volumes were published in the Undergraduate Prize Essays Series and two in the Scholars of the House Series. The authors of several of these essays have gone on to fulfill amply the promise of their early scholarly efforts. More recently the growing number of theses of outstanding merit has encouraged Yale College and the Yale University Press to establish this new YALE COLLEGE SERIES with the hope that every year it will be possible to publish some of the best work by the Honors majors in the Senior Class. The selection, which is necessarily a very rigorous one, was performed for the Class of 1964 by a faculty committee made up of Messrs. Martin Griffin, S. W. Reed, and E. M. Waith, Chairman.

Georges May
Dean of Yale College

To My Parents

ACKNOWLEDGMENTS

I am grateful to Robert Penn Warren, Martin Price, and James K. Folsom for reading and criticizing parts of this book. Above all, I am deeply indebted to Alvin B. Kernan for his tolerance, his understanding, and his critical judgment.

CONTENTS

1   EVELYN WAUGH

All over Evelyn Waugh's England country houses are being torn down. Hordes of men, well-trained in the art of demolition, arrive at magnificent estates, bringing with them the machines of destruction—monstrous steam shovels that undermine the most stubborn roots of culture, sledge hammers that shatter ancient rocks of tradition, grotesque iron claws that tear down the spires of religion. Nothing resists the onslaught; indeed, nature herself seems to assist, for entropy invades even the most sheltered and sacred preserves of order. Weeds spring up between cracks in the floors of ancestral halls, vines force themselves into weak points of chapel walls, mosquitoes and bats invade the life of quiet drawing rooms. The disintegrating world seems at the point of a great cataclysm, of the Second Coming even, but in this dying civilization there are neither resolutions nor revelations. The only being who arrives at the decaying and soon-to-be-destroyed manor houses is a small and rather unpleasant fellow, with canvas and brush, who wishes to record the old structures at the very moment of collapse.

Charles Ryder, the narrator of Waugh's novel *Brideshead Revisited,* is such a man. He describes himself as an "architectural painter," and proceeds to justify his choice of profession:

> I have always loved building, holding it to be not only the highest achievement of man but one in which, at the moment of consummation, things were most clearly taken out of his hands and perfected, without his intention, by other means, and I regarded men as something much less than the buildings they made and inhabited . . . After my first exhibition I was called to all parts of the country to make portraits of houses that were soon to be destroyed or debased; indeed, my arrival seemed often to be only a few paces ahead of the auctioneers, a presage of doom.[1]

1. Evelyn Waugh, *Brideshead Revisited* (London, 1944), p. 31. All citations of Waugh are to the standard edition published by Chapman and Hall, London.

For Charles Ryder, old houses are not merely piles of stone and mortar but symbols of all that is decent and worth while in the world. A fine, venerable English country estate stands, at once, for order, stability, goodness, civilization, and, above all, continuity with the past. Sanctified by time, "catching and keeping the best of each generation," such houses grow silently with the centuries, miraculously avoiding the filth of mankind. Men made the buildings, to be sure, but somehow, in the long process of accretion, men, with their pettiness and ugliness, have receded until they appear "as something much less than the buildings they made and inhabited, as mere lodgers and short-term sub-lesses of small importance in the long, fruitful life of their homes." Tragically, man's destructiveness cannot be put off forever, and the great homes are "rebuilt" in the nineteenth century and torn down in the twentieth to make way for apartment houses, factories, and insane asylums. Finally, all that is left of the grandeur and beauty of the centuries is a small canvas and a memory.

Evelyn Waugh, like Charles Ryder, is an architectural painter who sees, with anger, horror, and a kind of fascination, the destruction of old homes, the decay of institutions, the death of meaningful values. But Waugh refuses to create a merely sentimental picture of the achievements of the past at the moment of extinction; he insists, rather, upon recording in scrupulous detail the actual process of demolition. In Waugh's satiric vision, seemingly trivial events—the breaking up of a manor house, the redecoration of an old room with chromium plating, a drunken brawl in an Oxford courtyard—are symbols of a massive, irreversible, and terrifying victory of barbarism and the powers of darkness over civilization and light. Waugh's early novels, especially *Decline and Fall* (1928), *Vile Bodies* (1930), *Black Mischief* (1932), and *A Handful of Dust* (1934) are chronicles of that awful triumph.

The rebuilding and modernization of "the finest piece of domestic Tudor in England" (p. 130), in Waugh's first novel, *Decline and Fall,* is an image of everything that follows in Waugh's work and a symbol of the corruption of the whole society. Margot Beste-Chetwynde, a lovely socialite whose

chief source of income is the Latin-American Entertainment
Co., Ltd. (a vast chain of brothels in South America) buys
King's Thursday, a magnificent estate which has remained
almost wholly unchanged for three hundred years. There are
many inconveniences in a house without hot water and elec-
tricity, but the visitors and guests, returning in "their big
motor cars to their modernized manors" would reflect "how
they seemed to have been privileged to step for an hour and
a half out of their own century into the leisurely, prosaic
life of the English Renaissance" (p. 130). Such a glorious
anachronism cannot survive the twentieth century, however,
and Mrs. Beste-Chetwynde immediately contracts for a complete transformation of King's Thursday into "something
clean and square." The architect into whose hands is placed
this taxing and delicate commission is Professor Otto Fried-
rich Silenus, a brilliant young man whose previous works
had been a rejected design for a chewing-gum factory and the
"decor for a cinema film of great length and complexity of
plot—a complexity rendered the more inextricable by the
producer's austere elimination of all human characters."
The professor's theory of architecture is revealing and perfectly suited to his task:

> The problem of architecture as I see it . . . is the problem
> of all art—the elimination of the human element from
> the consideration of form. The only perfect building
> must be a factory, because that is built to house ma-
> chines, not men . . . Man is never beautiful; he is never
> happy except when he becomes the channel for the dis-
> tribution of mechanical forces.   [p. 136]

The good professor then must be serenely happy, for he has
overcome all traces of the human in himself. Pondering the
nature of art, "his fawn-like eyes were fixed and inexpressive,
and the hand which had held the biscuit still rose and fell
to and from his mouth with a regular motion, while his
empty jaws champed rhythmically; otherwise he was perfectly immobile" (p. 137).

Professor Silenus' success in rebuilding King's Thursday
in the modern style can only be fully appreciated in terms

of the tradition he has destroyed. The approach to the new house down the long avenue shaded by the budding chestnut trees through which the April sun infused a quiet radiance and serene beauty recalls the spirit of William Morris, reverently intoning a hymn of "seed time and harvest, the superb succession of the seasons, the harmonious interdependence of rich and poor, of dignity, innocence, and tradition" (p. 140). But the hymn is abruptly silenced at the end of the drive where the modern Pandemonium rises, a shining edifice of polished aluminum, vulcanite, malachite, and bottle-green vita-glass, inhabited by the beautiful owner of the Latin-American Entertainment Co., Ltd.

Professor Silenus is a ludicrous and comic figure, but he is also a man of genius, for he recognizes that modern man's answer to the problems of a complex and confusing existence is complete dehumanization, and accordingly he builds King's Thursday to accommodate not men but machines. Waugh's comment on modern society is hardheaded but not simple-minded. The modern building is vulgar and disgusting, a profanation of the past and a rejection of humanity, but the alternative is not to be found in the naïve sentimentality of the nineteenth century. Professor Silenus' notions are absurd, but so is the conviction that the "great chestnuts in the morning sun stood for something enduring and serene in a world that had lost its reason and would so stand when the chaos and confusion were forgotten" (p. 140). Chaos and confusion *are* the future for Waugh, and the destruction of the great Tudor manor was made possible by the weakness, flabbiness, and the naïveté of the Victorians. Blind faith in the beneficence of nature and the essential goodness of the soul is incapable of combating the savagery of the modern world. The chestnuts will be cut down for lumber to build the vast housing developments of the future.

The wholesale demolition of the value structures of the past and the creation in their place of a vile and absurd habitation is the central theme of Waugh's early novels. However, this theme does not always manifest itself in terms of a destroyed manor house. Man, in his fear and anxiety over the loss of values, unconsciously seeks dehumanization, but he may become a sort of animal as well as a machine. Waugh's description of the Llanabba Silver Band in *Decline and Fall* is a marvelously comic rendering of the theme of bestiality:

> They were low of brow, crafty of eye and crooked of limb. They advanced huddled together with the loping tread of wolves, peering about them furtively as they came, as though in constant terror of ambush; they slavered at their mouths, which hung loosely over their receding chins, while each clutched under his ape-like arm a burden of curious and unaccountable shape.
>
> [pp. 72–73]

The savage coexists perfectly with the streamlined man. While Otto Silenus is mechanically pondering a world inhabited by dynamos, Margot Beste-Chetwynde is procuring young girls for her brothels in South America; while brilliant debutantes and their beaux—the Bright Young People—are lost in an endless and dizzying round of parties, Basil Seal, in the jungles of Africa, is seated at a cannibal feast. Against the technological skill of the machine and the voracity of the savage, culture, refinement, and tradition have little defense. The jungle is always threatening to overrun the city, the work crews are always tearing down a country estate, and hordes of howling aristocrats and gate-crashers are always sullying the sacred preserves of order and decency.

Decline and Fall opens within the hallowed walls of Scone College, Oxford, where, instead of the hushed voices of serious scholars engaged in a discussion of the Classics, one hears "the sound of the English country families baying for broken glass" (p. 14), for it is the night of the annual Bollinger Club banquet. The club has a great tradition of savagery and merriment to uphold, for at the last meeting a fox had been brought in in a cage and stoned to death with champagne bottles, but the drunken crowd of epileptic royalty, illiterate lairds, and uncouth peers sustain their roles magnificently, breaking valuable china, smashing a grand piano, throwing a Matisse into a water jug, destroying manuscripts, breaking windows, and, finally, debagging an unsuspecting theology

7

student named Paul Pennyfeather who was returning from a most stimulating discussion of plebiscites in Poland. Two symbols of authority and responsibility, the Junior Dean and the Domestic Bursar, look down on the wild scene in delight, thinking of the prized port in the senior common-room that is only brought up when the college fines have reached fifty pounds. At a "lovely college meeting" the next morning, these fines are exacted, and, incidentally, the theology student, who ran the whole length of the quadrangle without his trousers, is expelled for indecent behavior.

Paul Pennyfeather, the young man so rudely thrust into the world, is singularly unsuited for its trials, for Paul is a shadow-man, completely passive, completely innocent. One of Waugh's favorite satiric devices is suddenly to catapult a totally naïve individual into a grotesque and uncontrollable world, for, with this technique, he can expose both the corruption of society and the hopelessness of naïve goodness and simple-minded humanism. Since the essence of Waugh's criticism of Paul Pennyfeather's innocence is that it is too simple to cope with the complexities of the world, one cannot expect complex character delineation, and indeed Paul's flatness is very carefully and successfully pursued. "Paul Pennyfeather would never have made a hero," Waugh blandly observes in the middle of the novel, "and the only interest about him arises from the unusual series of events of which his shadow was witness" (p. 139). This series of events begins, appropriately, at a crumbling castle, Waugh's symbol for dying values.

Llanabba Castle, a public school in Wales where Paul finds employment after his dismissal, is as much a sham as its proprietor and headmaster, Dr. Augustus Fagan, Esquire, Ph.D. The castle used to be plain Llanabba House, but it was made "formidably feudal" in the 1860s with the addition of a medieval façade and at least a mile of machicolated, crenelated, towered, and turreted wall "decorated with heraldic animals and a workable portcullis" (p. 26). The battlements are images of fortifications which earlier on the Welsh marshes might have found some use in the defense of a lonely outpost of civilization from hordes of barbarians, but, built at the time of the cotton famine in the '60s, they only served to satisfy the ridiculous pretensions and twisted ideals of the owner, a prosperous Lancashire mill owner. The castle is an absurd solution to an absurd moral dilemma— the owner's wife could not bear to think of their men starving, and the owner, having read the Liberal economists, could not bear to think of charity without tangible return. "Enlightened self-interest" found a resolution in the transformation of Llanabba House into Llanabba Castle—"a great deal of work had been done very cheaply" (p. 26). When Paul arrives at Llanabba, it is overrun by beastly little boys and disreputable adults, but the savages had already captured the house in the Victorian Age, for the wall, which had promised protection, was a sham and a perversion of meaningful values. After the enlightened mill owner with his twisted social and architectural values, the house is fit only for a movie set, a prison, or a public school.

Paul's experience at Llanabba is a marvelous initiation into the savagery of society, for all greed, corruption, doubt, ugliness, hysteria, and callous indifference to suffering are found there in microcosm. The butler, Solomon Philbrick, is a criminal; the schoolmaster, Captain Grimes, is a bigamist and a scroundel; the chaplain, Prendergast, is tormented by "doubts" and has no faith; the owner, Doctor Fagan, is a swindler. What Edmund Wilson calls "that hair-raising harlequinade in a brazenly bad boys' school"[2] is a comic tour de force in which Waugh proves his mastery of the technique of making insanity seem perfectly normal. All but the pretense of education and discipline is abandoned, as it is enormously difficult simply to prevent murder. Indeed, at the Annual School Sports, Prendergast shoots little Lord Tangent in the foot, an injury which later proves fatal.

Paul falls in love with Margot Beste-Chetwynde, the mother of one of his students, and moves from the Welsh countryside to sophisticated King's Thursday and London, but his experience is fundamentally the same. Once again, Pennyfeather is passive before the buffeting forces of fortune; once again he is surrounded by gross injustice, disloyalty,

2. Edmund Wilson, " 'Never Apologize, Never Explain': The Art of Evelyn Waugh," *Classics and Commercials* (New York, 1950), p. 141.

and chaos. Even the characters are the same—Solomon Philbrick is now managing director of a disreputable cinema company, Grimes is an employee of the Latin-American Entertainment Co., Ltd., Prendergast has become a "'Modern Churchman' who draws the full salary of a beneficed clergyman and need not commit himself to any religious belief" (p. 157). Sir Alastair Digby-Vaine-Trumpington, who debagged Paul back at Scone College, reappears as best man at Paul's wedding to Margot, a wedding prevented by Arthur Potts, Paul's best friend at Scone. Potts, now a League of Nations investigator, arrests Paul for connections with Margot's white slave enterprise. So Pennyfeather suffers another change of environment, this time to prison, where, of course, he meets Philbrick, Grimes, and Prendergast.

Sir Wilfred Lucas-Dockery, governor of Paul's new home, is a representative of the spirit of modern social reform and the new sociology. Believing that "almost all crime is due to the repressed desire for aesthetic expression" (p. 187), he issues carpenter's tools to a mystical maniac who promptly cuts off Mr. Prendergast's head. The murder of the Modern Churchman by the "Lion of the Lord's elect" (p. 198), the laying of absurd religious doubt by equally absurd religious conviction, is the sort of hilarious and gruesome irony Waugh delights in. The incident is typical in its audacity and its gratuitous cruelty, the latter a quality of Waugh's work which many readers have found disturbing. The grotesque, the unreasonable, and the cruel are always asserting themselves in the satirist's world—Miss Florence Ducane falls from the chandelier on which she has been swinging and kills herself, the Earl of Balcairn is a gossip columnist who writes his greatest story and then sticks his head in the gas oven, Basil Seal eats his girl friend at a cannibal banquet, a country gentleman's only child is kicked to death by a horse. The most outrageous events are reported with cavalier disregard. The amputation of Lord Tangent's gangrenous foot and his death, reported in widely separated and totally undramatic asides, are the source of great amusement in *Decline and Fall*. The deliberate accumulation of cruel details creates the atmosphere of a world where, as Eric Linklater observes, "the most monstrous injustice is as much a part of life as the early morning cup of tea."[3]

The traditional values have been brutally torn down with the country houses and replaced by mechanism and savagery, but there is a vital principle which has remained completely untouched by the change. This principle manifests itself in "the primitive promptings of humanity," epitomized by Captain Grimes, who, Paul muses, is one of the immortals:

> Surely he had followed in the Bacchic train of distant Arcady, and played on the reeds of myth by forgotten streams, and taught the childish satyrs the art of love? Had he not suffered unscathed the fearful dooms of all the offended gods of all the histories, fire, brimstone, and yawning earthquakes, plague and pestilence? Had he not stood, like the Pompeian sentry while the Citadels of the Plain fell to ruin about his ears? Had he not, like some grease-caked Channel swimmer, breasted the waves of the Deluge? Had he not moved unseen when darkness covered the waters? [pp. 221–22]

Grimes is a powerful life-force existing outside the pale of conventional morality, and, audacious, elusive, outrageous, free, he represents the spirit of *Decline and Fall*. The growth of Waugh's pessimism is reflected in his treatment of Grimes' spiritual heirs. Father Rothschild, S.J., in *Vile Bodies* and Krikor Youkoumian in *Black Mischief* are far less sympathetic, until, with Mrs. Beaver, in *A Handful of Dust,* the vital principle has become triumphant opportunism and moral blankness.

Paul Pennyfeather's excursion into society ends as abruptly as it began. Margot Beste-Chetwynde marries a vulgar but influential peer named Lord Metroland and arranges the hero's release from prison and his removal to a "High-class Nursing and Private Sanitorium" run by Augustus Fagan, M.D. Given a bogus death certificate, Paul returns to Oxford, in the guise of the cousin of deceased Pennyfeather, to resume his theological studies. The story has described a

3. Eric Linklater, *The Art of Adventure* (London, 1947), p. 46.

complete circle—in the last scene, Paul returns to his room, having attended a most stimulating discussion of plebiscites in Poland, and once again hears the "confused roaring and breaking of glass" of the Bollinger Club banquet. But Pennyfeather has at least profited slightly from his experience, for it is his friend Stubbs who makes the perilous journey back to his lodgings, while Paul settles back and reflects on the wisdom of the Early Church in suppressing heretics.

The plot of Evelyn Waugh's first novel is not a linear progression, a series of events which conclude in a true shift from the original condition, but a great circle "like the big wheel at Luna Park." Paul returns to his quiet and unreal existence at Scone, while outside his small room the English country families are once again baying for broken glass, King's Thursday is being torn down and rebuilt yet another time, Margot Metroland is encouraging more young girls to "take a place" in South America, Solomon Philbrick is tearing about in an open Rolls-Royce, Dr. Fagan has published a best-seller entitled *Mother Wales*. The order which appeared to have been restored is wholly illusory, condemnation of heretics is long past, the wonderful Tudor house can never be rebuilt.

Paul Pennyfeather was caught up in the mad tarantella of society yet managed to remain always aloof and finally to escape with nothing worse than a hard bump, but Adam Fenwick-Symes, the hero of Waugh's next novel, *Vile Bodies*, is totally imprisoned in the world of the Bright Young People. He is trapped in a streamlined inferno where the reason no longer controls lust, where people dance madly in meaningless circles and shout convulsively "Faster, faster," where not only are all traditions and institutions abandoned as sham, but life itself is "too, too bogus." Adam, his fiancée Nina Blount, and his friends Agatha Runcible, Miles Malpractice, Ginger Littlejohn, and Archie Schwert are completely rootless, lost in a world where there is no longer good or evil, sin or redemption, but only a ghastly ennui. *Decline and Fall* was characterized by its wild audacity, but *Vile Bodies* is a comedy haunted by an inexplicable sadness. The flickering of awareness in Adam and of love in Nina only intensifies the pathos of wasted lives:

> ". . . Nina, do you ever feel that things simply can't go on much longer?"
> "What d'you mean by things—us or everything?"
> "Everything."
> . . . Later he said: "I'd give anything in the world for something different."
> "Different from me or different from everything?"
> "Different from everything . . . only I've got nothing . . . what's the good of talking?"
> "Oh, Adam, my dearest . . ."
> "Yes?"
> "Nothing." [p. 185]

One of the curious qualities of *Vile Bodies* is the reader's inability to discriminate between guilt and innocence. In *Decline and Fall* Paul Pennyfeather was clearly an innocent suddenly thrown into a corrupt world, but the distinction is blurred in *Vile Bodies*. Adam sells his fiancée for £78 16s. 2d. and is an adulterer, but at the same time he exhibits an extraordinary naïveté and innocence, for he is conscious of breaking no moral norms.

Vile Bodies is an experimental novel. There is practically no plot and no continuity of narrative. The scenes shift wildly from the stormy English Channel to a party given for Mrs. Melrose Ape, the noted evangelist; from the intrigues of Father Rothschild, S.J., and the Prime Minister Walter Outrage to the small talk of two middle-class ladies on a train; from the drawing room of a huge mansion to the grease pit at the auto races. With this technique of disconnected and seemingly irrelevant scenes, Waugh is attempting to portray a world that is chaotic and out of joint. Readers have complained, with some justification, that the technique is all too successful, that the novel is disjointed and slights the affairs of Adam Fenwick-Symes and Nina Blount; but *Vile Bodies* is not a love story. Adam and Nina are significant only as representatives of the sickness of an entire generation, and their thwarted attempt to marry is meaningful and in-

13

teresting only as a symbol of the frustrated search for values of all the Bright Young People.

The central image of *Vile Bodies* is the delirious dream of Agatha Runcible, who had drunkenly stepped into an idling racing car and cracked up after a few wild spins around the track:

> I thought we were driving round and round in a motor race and none of us could stop, and there was an enormous audience composed entirely of gossip writers and gate crashers . . . and people like that, all shouting at us at once to go faster. [p. 181]

Waugh prefaces his novel with a quotation from *Through the Looking Glass* which sets the dominant tone of breathless futility in *Vile Bodies:* "it takes all the running you can do, to keep in the same place." Round and round the Bright Young People go in an endless circle of parties—"Masked parties, Savage parties, Victorian parties, Greek parties, Wild West parties, Russian parties, Circus parties . . ." (p. 118)—and all their trivial affairs are duly reported by the eighth Earl of Balcairn, Viscount Erdinge, Baron Cairn of Balcairn, Red Knight of Lancaster, Count of the Holy Roman Empire and Chenonceaux Herald to the Duchy of Aquitaine, who is a gossip columnist for the *Daily Excess.*

The fate of the old order with its decency, culture, and stability is represented by the fate of Anchorage House, the last survivor of the noble town houses of London. This mansion was, in its time, of dominating and august dimensions, but now "it had become a mere 'picturesque bit' lurking in a ravine between concrete skyscrapers." The house and the values for which it stands, the values of those "people of decent and temperate life, uncultured, unaffected, unembarrassed, unassuming, unambitious people, of independent judgment and marked eccentricities" (p. 121), have not diminished in worth, but they are stifled and dwarfed by the sterile culture of the modern age. A party at Anchorage House, "anchored" in custom and tradition, is juxtaposed with an orgy held by the Bright Young People in a dirigible, and the loss of the firm ground of the past is painfully obvious.

The younger generation is plagued by "radical instability," but this disease is largely the result of their parents' stupidity, deceitfulness, and viciousness. Religion is represented by Father Rothschild, S.J., whose small suitcase of imitation crocodile hide contains the tools of international intrigue, and by Mrs. Melrose Ape, the woman evangelist, whose "angels" sing unceasingly the inspiring hymn "There Ain't No Flies on the Lamb of God." The state is in the unsteady hands of the Right Honorable Walter Outrage, M.P., who must inquire, after the euphoric dreams induced by a large dose of chloral, if he is still Prime Minister. The feminine world oscillates between "those two poles of savagery" (p. 110)—Lady Circumference, uncouth and vulgar, and Lady Metroland, proprietress of the Latin-American Entertainment Co., Ltd. And the control of art is the domain of the customs officials who self-righteously proclaim, "If we can't stamp out literature in the country, we can at least stop its being brought in from outside" (p. 23), and of rapacious publishers who demand a "very straightforward arrangement" amounting to complete peonage for the author.

Adam seeks to acquire enough money to marry Nina, but all his attempts are maddeningly thwarted. His autobiography is burned by customs; Nina's father, Colonel Blount, gives him a check for a thousand pounds which is signed "Charlie Chaplin"; a Major who owes Adam 35,000 pounds is always too drunk or too elusive to deliver the money. Finally Nina despairs and marries a repulsive but wealthy gentleman named Ginger Littlejohn. Their honeymoon, at a "top-hole little spot not far from Monte with a very decent nine-hole golf course," is a ghastly failure, and Adam and Nina resume their affair at her father's estate, pronounced Doubting 'All by the servants. The house, with its lofty Palladian façade, fronted by an equestrian statue pointing a baton imperiously down the main drive, promises order and sanity, but Colonel Blount, the owner, is a senile eccentric who lets his estate to The Wonderfilm Company of Great Britain for the filming of the life of John Wesley. Under the direction of a Mr. Isaacs and starring Effie La Touche, the company makes "the most important all-talking super-religious film to be produced solely in this country by British artists and management and by British capital" (p. 124). The movie, with its futile hyperactivity, its absurdity, and its falseness, mirrors the life of the Bright Young People, and the film's technique—a breathless succession of unrelated scenes and the peculiarity "that whenever the story reached a point of dramatic and significant action, the film seemed to get faster and faster" (p. 203)—parodies Waugh's own style in the novel.

From Doubting Hall the scene shifts, appropriately, to the "biggest battlefield in the history of the world" (p. 212), where Adam, seated on a splintered tree stump, surveys the desolate expanse of mud in which every visible object has been burnt or broken. No positive value has survived the corrosive force of doubt, boredom, cynicism, and dullness. All ideals, all morality, all culture have been destroyed, and, at home, the gossip writers, the boors, the infernal machines, and the savages hold illimitable dominion over all.

Black Mischief seems, at first, a rather sudden and unexpected departure from *Decline and Fall* and *Vile Bodies*. Waugh's third novel opens not in an Oxford quadrangle or a Mayfair town house but in Azania, "a large imaginary island off the East Coast of Africa, in character and history a combination of Zanzibar and Abyssinia."[4] Waugh draws heavily on his personal experiences and observations in Abyssinia as a foreign correspondent; indeed much of the fine description in the novel seems transposed from his travel book *Remote People* (1931). But *Black Mischief* is not a witty travelogue or, as some readers have felt, a vicious, racist attack on the African Negro. Rather, it treats precisely the themes of the earlier works—the shabbiness of Western culture, the decline and fall of institutions, the savagery underlying society.

Black Mischief chronicles the attempted modernization of

4. Waugh, quoted in Frederick J. Stopp, *Evelyn Waugh* (Boston, 1958), p. 77.

a black nation by Seth, "Emperor of Azania, Chief of Chiefs of Sakuyu, Lord of Wanda and Tyrant of the Seas, Bachelor of the Arts of Oxford University" (p. 9). As his title indicates, Seth's character is a paradoxical blend of savagery and civilization, the cannibal feast and the drawing room. He is unpredictable, cruel, naïve, insanely optimistic, lonely, terrified. He insists that he is the New Age, the Future, "Light and Speed and Strength, Steel and Steam, Youth, Today and To-morrow" (p. 41). But at night, in the darkness of his palace, "the acquired loneliness of civilization" joins with the "inherited terror of the jungle" (p. 28) to reduce the Apostle of Modernity to a shivering, whimpering infant. Seth's modernity, however, is not a meaningless label or a thin veneer of culture concealing the dominating violence of his black soul, for the meaning of *Black Mischief* is not the impossibility of civilizing the Negro. That the ideal of Progress in which Seth so fervently believes turns out to be a shabby concatenation of inane conventions is a condemnation far more of the cultivated Westerner than of the African. Seth serves the artistic purpose of a Paul Pennyfeather: he is a naïve outsider who, in his contact with an alien society, is the means of satirizing that society.

Seth's cohort and adviser in the attempted reconstruction of the empire is a Bright Young Person named Basil Seal. Like Adam Fenwick-Symes, Seal is both innocent and corrupt, his personality well reflected in his characteristic expression, which is "insolent, sulky, and curiously childish" (p. 121). At Oxford, where Seth was classed among "Bengali babus, Siamese and grammar school scholars" (p. 109), Basil stood for the impressionable young ruler as the "personification of all that glittering, intangible Western culture to which he aspired" (p. 109). When Basil, disgusted with the boredom of London society, travels to Azania, Seth finds the representative of Progress and the New Age for whom he has been longing. Seal is at once appointed head of the Ministry of Modernization, and the One Year Plan commences.

Just as Basil Seal, intelligent, unprincipled, and curiously naïve, represents the new breed of Englishmen, so His Britannic Majesty's Minister to Azania, Sir Samson Courte-

17

ney, foolish, bumbling, and incapable, represents the older generation. Inside the Legation, "a miniature garden city in a stockaded compound" (p. 49), the envoy, his wife, and daughter Prudence live a sheltered existence of croquet, afternoon tea, and poorly played bridge. The sad fate of the British Raj is eloquently reflected in the minister's favorite pastime—playing in the bathtub with an inflated india-rubber sea-serpent. Prudence Courteney, preoccupied with sex and romance, spends her time writing an adolescent "Panorama of Life" and nourishing her infatuation first for William, the assistant attaché, and then for Basil. The remainder of the diplomatic community consists of Mr. Schonbaum, a rich American of uncertain lineage, and M. Ballon, the stock Frenchman whose character is totally expressed by his Freemasonry and flair for melodrama ("he was keeping the last cartridge for Madame Ballon," p. 53).

The abortive attempt to modernize Azania is not a statement of the African nation's inability to share in the glories of civilization but a sly and satiric examination of modernity itself. The struggle which Seth envisages as a mortal combat between barbarism and Progress is a miserable sham, for Western culture itself is no longer meaningful. Those Western ideas which might have given Seth's project real significance have been abandoned. Basil informs Seth:

> "We've got a much easier job now than we should have had fifty years ago. If we'd had to modernize a country then it would have meant constitutional monarchy, bicameral legislature, proportional representation, women's suffrage, independent judicature, freedom of the press, referendums . . ."
> "What is all that?" asked the Emperor.
> "Just a few ideas that have ceased to be modern."
>
> [p. 127]

Instead, modernity consists of a tank which the natives use as a torture chamber; boots, which the natives eat; contraception, which the natives call "the Emperor's juju" and believe will ensure them immense families. Modernity is a

18

new palace constructed of steel and vita-glass (the materials used by Professor Silenus in rebuilding King's Thursday), Nacktkultur, bogus paper money, and refined techniques of cruelty to animals. The inspiring motto "Through Sterility to Culture" is the banner not merely of the participants in the birth-control pageant but of the entire European civilization. Western culture is sterile, totally isolated from the realities of human life and incapable of making man's existence more pleasant.

Waugh uses Africa as a lens which renders grotesque and revealing images of English institutions and social classes. The Bright Young People and their silly parents, scheming politicians and unscrupulous soldiers of fortune, crude peers and nouveau riche socialites are all represented in the Azanian court. The reforming zeal of Sir Wilfred Lucas-Dockery is revived in the marvelous comic figure Dame Mildred Porch, who comes to Azania to crusade for more humane treatment of animals. And as Sir Wilfred's humanitarian theories of criminal behavior provided a homicidal maniac with carpenter's tools, Dame Mildred's species of folly conceals a comic vein of cruelty and inhuman stupidity. "Fed doggies in market place," she writes to her husband, "Children tried to take food from doggies. Greedy little wretches" (p. 155). Captain Grimes, carrier of the immortal life-force in *Decline and Fall,* is reincarnated as Krikor Youkoumian, the Armenian merchant, who cultivates the age-old art of cheating the government and avoiding "bust-ups." The uncouth noblemen who unleash their savagery at Bollinger Club banquets appear, in *Black Mischief,* as the Earl of Ngumo and his company, attired in lion skins and hopelessly drunk. Nor does Azanian society lack corrupt peers and scheming priests who lust for money and power and seek to overthrow the government. The plot of Viscount Boaz and the Nestorian patriarch to depose Seth is the African equivalent of the machinations of Father Rothschild and Mr. Outrage in *Vile Bodies.* Waugh, then, does not turn away from England at all in *Black Mischief.* Rather, the black faces and foreign dress heighten the ironic force of Waugh's biting scrutiny of his homeland.

As *Decline and Fall* was signalized by its comic audacity
and *Vile Bodies* by its comic sadness, *Black Mischief* is characterized by its comic cruelty. Recurring references, quite
hilarious in their context, to starving children, executed men,
and mutilated bodies constantly remind the reader that as
Seth's blind infatuation with Western culture grows, the
savagery underlying the calm surface of the superimposed
civilization becomes increasingly agitated until it explodes
in a revolt which overthrows the Emperor. Seth and Basil
flee into the jungle, where the Emperor is killed by the
treacherous Viscount Boaz who is in turn killed by the
treacherous Major Joab. Basil orders the natives to "kill
your best meat and prepare a feast in the manner of your
people" (p. 220), and the great funeral banquet begins. As
the feast progresses, the native dances grow more and more
violent, until blood and sweat stream from the frenzied
witch doctors and tribesmen who make a human chain
around the funeral pyre, "shuffling their feet and heaving
their shoulders, spasmodically throwing back their heads and
baying like wild beasts" (p. 223). Suddenly, Basil recognizes
on the head of the native chief the red beret that Prudence
Courteney wore as she was leaving Azania to return to London. Horrified, he asks the chief where the white woman is.
The headman grunts drunkenly and replies: " 'Why, here,'
he patted his distended paunch. 'You and I and the big chiefs
—we have just eaten her' " (p. 224). The jungle's triumph
over civilization is complete.

Waugh's delight in architectural images does not diminish
in *Black Mischief*. The tough, old Anglican Cathedral in
Debra Dowa, that impractical and "shocking ugly building,"
is marked for demolition by Seth and the Ministry of
Modernization to make way for the Place Marie Stopes. But
the Cathedral, despite its many years of disuse, has a remarkable solidity, and, as the contractor in charge of the destruction remarks, "It's not any one's job breaking up that
Cathedral. Solid granite shipped all the way from Aberdeen"
(p. 151). Just before the revolt which ends his reign, Seth
himself, wearing an elegant gray suit and parti-colored shoes,
batters in desperation at the granite archway of the structure

which symbolizes resistance to the new order. The attempt to replace the worship of God with the worship of Progress is even more obvious in the site of the Ministry of Modernization, which occupies what had formerly been the old Empress' oratory.

Seth's palace compound, like the concept of progress it embodies, is a haphazard conglomeration of strange structures, refuse, and, occasionally, the flyblown carcase of a donkey or camel. Modernity and barbarism are linked in the grand work-projects of leveling and draining which are pursued without any success by gangs of prisoners chained neck to neck. The headquarters of the One Year Plan, likewise, stands between a slaughtering block and a "minor gallows for such trivial, domestic executions as now and then became necessary within the royal household" (p. 117). In spite of the bright posters that are supposed to give the casual onlooker a feeling of exhilaration and religious confidence in Progress, the Ministry of Modernization is a desolate structure, often deserted except for a single dog "who gnawed her hindquarters in the patch of shadow cast by two corpses which rotated slowly face to face, half circle East, a half circle west, ten foot high in the limpid morning sunlight" (p. 117).

The sense of desolation and decay is best conveyed, however, by another structure—a wrecked automobile, lying in the middle of the Avenue of Progress, its tires devoured by white ants, its motor removed by pilfering, its rusting body reinforced by rags, tin, mud, and grass and used as a home by a native family. The rotting car appears throughout *Black Mischief* as an impediment which Seth tries in vain to remove, and, at the end of the novel, when the British and French hold Azania as a joint protectorate, it is still blocking traffic, unmoved by the entire force of the League of Nations.

Seth's deposition and murder seems to be the laying of the ghost of madness and instability. The protectorate, with its pukka sahibs, police stations, snobbery, European clubs, polished brass, and Gilbert and Sullivan, promises to be a grand step forward in the onward March of Progress, but, like the reign of Seth, it is a ridiculous sham. Basil Seal has

returned to the jungles of London, Youkoumian is still sell-
ing junk to the government, the natives still massacre each
other beyond the walls of the city, impoverished Arabs still
saunter hand in hand by the sea wall discussing very old
problems of litigation and remarking sadly that Azania is
no longer a gentleman's country. The history of Azania, like
the dance of the witch doctors and the life of the Bright
Young People, is a savage, futile, comic circle.

In *A Handful of Dust* Waugh returns to England to tell
a seemingly simple story of the failure of a marriage. Tony
Last, a country gentleman, lives with his lovely wife, Brenda,
and only son, John Andrew, at Hetton, a large ancestral
estate which the county guide book notes "was entirely rebuilt in 1864 in the Gothic style and is now devoid of interest" (p. 8). For Tony, however, the house, with all its inconveniences and its charms, its antiquated heating apparatus and bedrooms named Morgan le Fay and Guinevere, is
the most delightful place on earth, and he is perfectly content to spend his entire life at Hetton in isolation from the
savage London Society. Brenda, on the contrary, finds both
home and husband terribly dull, and without the least
thought or concern she has an affair with a totally uninteresting young man named John Beaver. When Tony's only
child is killed in a hunting accident and Brenda reveals her
infidelity, Tony's "whole Gothic world had come to grief" (p.
163), and he wanders off to Brazil to meet a bizarre fate at the
hand of a lunatic. Brenda marries Tony's best friend, and
a family of impoverished Lasts turn Hetton into a silver-fox
farm. What might have been a rather dull "bedroom farce,"
however, is transformed by Waugh into a terrifying and
bitter examination of humanism and modern society, which
is the culmination of his art.

A Handful of Dust opens not at Hetton but "Du Coté de
Chez Beaver," in the mean little house inhabited by John
Beaver and his "mumsey," an interior decorator. The Beavers
are devoted to each other, nasty, parasitical, and unbearably
dull. Beaver is a villain, but he lacks all sense of pleasure in
the active pursuit of evil, of self-affirmation in immoral acts,

of life in cruel behavior. His atrocities have none of the flair of a Basil Seal or a Krikor Youkoumian but are rather passive and sad. Even the quality of consummate viciousness is lost in this moribund society! Beaver lives by perpetually sponging on others, and he announces to his mother that this week end's unsuspecting host is to be Tony Last. With the omniscience of a Father Rothschild, she analyzes the Lasts quite accurately: "She's lovely, he's rather a stick . . . I should say it was time she began to be bored. They've been married five or six years" (pp. 3–4). To this appraisal is added, later in the chapter, the comment of Tony's best friend, Jock Grant-Menzies: "I often think Tony Last's one of the happiest men I know. He's got just enough money, loves the place, one son he's crazy about, devoted wife, not a worry in the world" (p. 7).

With these two perspectives and with the knowledge that Beaver is about to enter the life of Tony and Brenda Last, we now move to idyllic Hetton and the wonderful description of the house and grounds. By the accumulation of a great many seemingly irrelevant details, Waugh evokes a whole world, a philosophy, and a way of life as well as an architecture and a landscape. Hetton is a lovely, sentimental, idealized world of the past and of childhood, at once silly and charming, hopelessly naïve and endearing. Far in the past Hetton had been an abbey, but, as religion receded, it became "one of the notable houses of the country" (p. 8), and, finally, in the nineteenth century, at the height of the Gothic revival, this structure was totally demolished and the present house was built as a monument to Victorian aesthetics. If the true significance and beauty of Hetton had been destroyed in 1864 or earlier when it ceased to shelter pious monks, at least the glazed brick and encaustic tile of the present structure have a character and sentimental worth completely lacking in the cold, oversize boxes being constructed in London. In the twentieth century, however, the huge building, with battlements and towers, a huge clock with maddeningly loud chimes, lancet windows of armorial stained glass, pitch-pine minstrels' gallery, Gothic bedrooms, moldy tapestries, and a fireplace resembling a thirteenth-century tomb, is rather impractical, mildly uncomfortable, and completely unfashionable.

Like the house itself, Hetton's proprietor, Tony Last, is a simple-minded creature of the past who has never quite grown up:

> Morgan le Fay had always been his room since he left the night nursery. He had been put there so that he would be in calling distance of his parents, inseparable in Guinevere; for until late in his life he was subject to nightmare. [p. 10]

This passage, typical of Waugh's technique of submerged import, suggests Tony's immaturity and his primal fear of the real nature of things. Tony's parents were inseparable, but Tony and Brenda sleep in separate bedrooms, Tony only one step beyond the night nursery and Brenda in a room named for a woman famed for her infidelity. Tony's nightmares look forward to his delirium and the nightmarish ending in Brazil, when the terrible fears of childish fantasy suddenly become real. *A Handful of Dust* bristles with such ironic and ambiguous details. Brenda "had insisted on a modern bed" in the midst of the old, traditional bedroom, John Andrew's horse is named after "a strawberry roan called Thunderclap who killed two riders," Beaver interrupts "the simple, mildly ceremonious order" of Tony's Sunday morning. When Brenda remarks to her husband that "Beaver isn't so bad. He's quite like us in some ways," Tony replies, "He's not like me" (p. 32). The lack of communication between Brenda and Tony becomes a clear rift when Brenda tells Beaver that she really detests Hetton: "I shouldn't feel so badly about it if it were really a lively house —like my home for instance . . . but of course Tony's been brought up here and sees it all differently" (p. 34). When, on a periodic trip to London, Brenda becomes Beaver's mistress, there is no surprise and practically no explanation.

The infidelity and the disintegration of the marriage are not analyzed in terms of the characters' deep, personal drives or romantic love or even blind lust. Brenda cherishes no illusions about her chosen lover: "He's second rate and a snob, and, I should think, as cold as a fish, but I happen to have a fancy for him, that's all" (p. 51). There are no soul-searchings, no tortured moments of guilt, no remorseful thoughts of home and family. Brenda's choice of John Beaver is completely thoughtless and completely appropriate, for they inhabit a world and share a set of values about which Tony Last, content at Hetton, can know nothing.

The complete absence of any emotional life in the characters of Waugh's satires has irritated certain critics. Graham Martin complains that "when we explore for the real substance of the marriage and its breakdown, try to realize the motives and the sympathies of the wife, lover, and husband, as the seriousness of their situation appears to invite us, we run up against a blank silence."[5] But one must not ask Evelyn Waugh or any satirist for a deep psychological examination of his characters, for this would be inimical to the satire itself. Satire, like comedy, is bound to be directed at the nonpersonal and mechanistic, for it sees man as an automaton, swept up in the mad conventions of society. Bergson's formula of the comic—"something mechanical encrusted on the living"[6]—applies to the satiric as well, where characters are usually flat, mindless, unaware, mechanical. At the moment when a character becomes aware of the web of folly or madness which is suffocating him, or when he suddenly turns in upon himself and sees with horror the corruption which is destroying his soul, then satire has been abandoned and the realm of tragedy is entered. Satiric detachment can only be maintained when characters are soulless actors in a social drama, when the author treats his creations not as individuals with private lives but as symbols of societal forces. Any single character taken out of this context and forced to stand naked before the critic will naturally seem flat and unreal, but this individual emptiness is not a symptom of what Martin calls Waugh's "brilliant faking."[7]

5. Graham Martin, "Novelists of Three Decades: Evelyn Waugh, Graham Greene, C. P. Snow," *The Modern Age,* Pelican Guide to English Literature, 7 (Baltimore, 1961), 400.
6. Henri Bergson, "Laughter," in *Comedy* (Garden City, 1956), p. 84.
7. Martin, p. 400.

Rather it is the result of an attempt to portray characters who have lost their inner beings, their complexity, their moral and intellectual independence. The satirist's careful and quite conscious shrinking of his characters' personalities does not mean, however, that satire must deal with trivialities, for, seen in his proper ambient, Tony Last transcends a shallow characterization of a sap and becomes the complex symbol of a dying value system at once hopelessly naïve and deeply sympathetic, unable to cope with society and yet the last spark of human decency in a vile world.

Waugh's brilliance and the source of his bitter pessimism is his remarkable ability to sustain an ironic double vision, to laugh uproariously at his posing, lying, stupid, carnal, vicious, and unhappy characters at the same time that he is leading them on to damnation through those very qualities. The plot of *A Handful of Dust* is very much that of a typical bedroom farce—the stupid country squire with the beautiful wife is cuckolded by a young man from the city—and Waugh does not hesitate to employ all the stock devices of such comedy. The husband, now called "old boy" by his friends, is the only person in the world who does not know of his wife's affair. The clever wife treats her husband outrageously and then makes him feel guilty for being such a suspicious old fool. Assignations are kept right under the husband's nose, to the delight of all informed onlookers. Old maids and matronly ladies get immense vicarious pleasure from the affair, which they treat as a marvelous fairy story of an imprisoned princess rescued by a shining hero. But the unrestrained laughter with which the reader is conditioned to greet such situations is never wholly fulfilled, for the reader is aware of the double vision, of the bitterly ironic and unforgiving theme underlying the surface gaiety and flamboyance.

The essence of Waugh's brilliant yoking of the comic and the satiric can be seen in the grotesque sermons delivered by Reverend Tendril, the vicar of Tony's church. The Vicar, it seems, had composed his sermons while serving in India and had neglected to adapt them to the changed conditions of his ministry. His traditional Christmas message is a delightful and revealing absurdity:

> "How difficult it is for us," he began, blandly surveying his congregation, who coughed into their mufflers and chafed their chilblains under their woolen gloves, "to realize that this is indeed Christmas. Instead of the glowing log fire and the windows tight shuttered against the drifting snow, we have only the harsh glare of the alien sun; instead of the happy circle of loved faces, of home and family, we have the uncomprehending stares of the subjected, though no doubt grateful heathen. Instead of the placid ox and ass of Bethlehem," said the vicar, slightly losing the thread of his comparisons, "we have for companions and the ravening tiger and the exotic camel, the furtive jackel and the ponderous elephant..."
>
> [p. 61]

Superficially, the Vicar's sermon is a charming and clever employment of the Bergsonian image of the mechanical encrusted on the living. Reverend Tendril, in his comic rigidity, is unable to adapt to fluid and mobile existence and delivers a sermon which seems completely divorced from reality. But the comic device only partially obscures the symbolic reality which the vicar has inadvertently reached. In spite of the illusion of security, Tony Last is indeed in a jungle, blinded by the harsh glare of an alien sun, surrounded by predatory animals. Hetton is not an impregnable bastion of humanity and happiness in a hostile world; it is a house defenseless against the ravening tiger. These symbolic meanings are never forced on the reader, however, but always remain cunningly concealed beneath the surface humor. Often, in fact, the import of an ironic remark is never fully grasped by the reader, remaining rather on a subconscious plane. A casual reference to a modern bed or a horse that killed three riders is ironically recalled two hundred pages later in the novel, not with the expectation that the reader will consciously remember precisely the earlier remark but with the purpose of giving the novel continuity and depth.

Waugh's world is one in which the worst possible events implicit in any situation can and do happen, a world where the savagery underlying a seemingly innocent remark is always fully realized. Basil Seal's endearment, "Prudence . . . I'd like to eat you," comes true, of course, at a cannibal feast. Tony Last's flippant remark, "I hope [John Andrew] . . . doesn't break his neck," is followed, that same afternoon, by his son's death. *A Handful of Dust* is a novel filled with improbable events and grotesque characters, but nothing ever happens for which the reader is not thoroughly prepared by Waugh. Even the fantastic ending in the jungles of Brazil is foreshadowed in the Vicar's Christmas sermon, and, though the reader may never consciously make the connection, the logic of the finale has been established. If we characterize Waugh's first three novels as comic audacity, comic sadness, and comic cruelty respectively, *A Handful of Dust* may be understood as comic bitterness, the comedy of rigidity and misunderstanding, the bitterness of betrayed ideals and fallen dreams.

The "ravening tiger and the exotic camel" arrive at Hetton by train, at Brenda's invitation, soon after Christmas. Mrs. Beaver, whose rapaciousness exceeds that of any jungle beast, decides that Hetton can only be made habitable by covering the walls with white chromium plating and laying natural sheepskin carpets, improvements which she will be more than glad to arrange. The exotic camel is Jenny Abdul Akbar, a revolting "princess" with whom, Brenda hopes, Tony is to have an affair that will keep him busy. Even Tony, however, has enough sense and good taste to laugh at Jenny, whose endless prattle about her former husband, the Moulay ("a beautiful and a very bad man"), is as counterfeit as the London society in which she thrives. Brenda, though, is somewhat consoled, for she has now done "far more than most wives would to cheer the old boy up" (p. 97). Tony's charming little world is clearly disintegrating, and the horse which fatally kicks John Andrew in the head is simply following a logic of chaos and blind cruelty in nature equivalent to that in society.

In his reaction to the child's death, Tony reveals the ter-

rible price he has paid for his simple-minded humanism, for
he has lost the ability to assert his identity even in the moment of greatest suffering. In complete abnegation, Tony
worries about everyone's feelings but his own:

> there's got to be an inquest the doctor says. It's purely
> formal of course, but it will be ghastly for that Ripon
> girl. . . . It's going to be so much worse for Brenda. You
> see she's got nothing else, much, except John. I've got
> her, and I love the house . . . but with Brenda John al-
> ways came first . . . And then you know she's seen so
> little of John lately. She's been in London such a lot . . .
> I know Brenda so well.   [pp. 113–16]

Tony, ignorant, self-deceived, and unknowingly referring to
John Beaver, is pitiable here, but he is certainly not a tragic
or even a wholly sympathetic figure. By constantly denying
his own feelings, he has gradually reduced himself to a cipher.
The fantasy world into which he had retreated to avoid the
mechanical, dehumanized society has, ironically, robbed him
of his humanity. "It's a pity you don't play patience," says
a card-playing friend to Tony, but Tony's whole life is an
absurd game of patience without solution, without end.

The fatal hunting accident removes the last, fragile link
between the worlds of Tony and Brenda, and Brenda's letter,
a few days later, asking for a divorce, is a mere formality for
everyone but Tony, who had "got into a habit of loving and
trusting" (p. 134) his wife. Tony's habits and illusions are
systematically destroyed during the divorce proceedings,
which are a monstrous perversion of values and meaning.
"It was thought convenient that Brenda should appear as the
plaintiff," and so Tony goes through the elaborate farce of
an adulterous week end at the seaside with a prostitute who
brings her *enfant terrible* along with her. The whole intricate and reassuring order of Tony's life has been destroyed:

> For a month now he had lived in a world suddenly
> bereft of order; it was as though the whole reasonable
> and decent constitution of things, the sum of all he had

experienced or learned to expect, were an inconspicuous, inconsiderable object mislaid somewhere on the dressing table; no outrageous circumstance in which he found himself, no new mad thing brought to his notice could add a jot to the all-encompassing chaos that shrieked about his ears. [p. 147]

This total disintegration recalls the mad banquet of Trimalchio in the *Satyricon* and the "universal Darkness" in the *Dunciad;* it is the vision of hell which has tormented every great satirist and which underlies all of Waugh's early work.

When Tony is informed that Brenda wishes him to sell Hetton in order to buy Beaver for her, he is shocked into a brief moment of clarity: "A whole Gothic world had come to grief . . . there was now no armour glittering in the forest glades, no embroidered feet on the greensward; the cream and dappled unicorns had fled . . ." (p. 163). Tony has moved from illusory security to chaos, a habit of love to despair, a life of meaning to devastating emptiness.

But without his illusions, Tony ceases to exist, and so he is compelled to wander in search of his lost city. Tony calls himself an explorer, but he is, in reality, an anti-explorer, for he is trying desperately to escape the unknown. His fantastic, shadowy guide, Dr. Messinger, has told Tony that the city is located in the Brazilian jungle and is called by the natives "the Shining, the Many-Watered, the Bright Feathered, the Aromatic Jam" (p. 172), but Tony already knows exactly what it will look like:

It was Gothic in character, all vanes and pinnacles, gargoyles, battlements, groining and tracery, pavilions and terraces, a transfigured Hetton, pennons and banners floating on the sweet breeze, everything luminous and translucent; a coral citadel crowning a green hill top sewn with daisies, among graves and streams; a tapestry landscape filled with heraldic and fabulous animals and symmetrical, disproportionate blossom.

[pp. 172–73]

The lost city is that fairyland for which Tony has always longed, that world without evil or death or unhappiness or people, that radiant sanctuary of stability and saccharine truth in the midst of a chaotic universe.

Tony's distant ancestors might have sought a hardheaded, human solution to the problems of unidealized existence, but the family line has gone sour and Tony is heir to the rottenness, imbecility, and sham of his nineteenth-century forebears who tore down a noble house to build a pretentious and fraudulent structure in its place. Faced with the realities of human viciousness and supported by nothing but his useless humanism, Tony can only retreat into infantile fantasies. Dr. Messinger, however, is not the agent of fairyland who leads Tony to the lost city of his dreams, but a Charon who conducts his charge into the hell which lay hidden behind the façades of civilization. The repeated juxtaposition of a scene in Brazil and a similar scene in London makes devastatingly clear Waugh's point that the foul, inhuman jungle in which Tony wanders feverishly is London transfigured. At the heart of darkness, the intricate and elaborate screen of lies with which modern man comforts himself is torn away, and the horror and savagery of society is laid bare. Here, in a world where the distinction between reality and nightmare has broken down, the inhabitants are avaricious, moronic, superstitious, insolent cannibals; reason can no longer control passion; nature is cruel and treacherous; exposed flesh is prey to the bloodsucking thirst of vampire bats and malarial mosquitoes.

Fever-ridden and raving, Tony at last grasps the whole of his life as a grotesque hallucination. In a remarkable and brilliant passage, all of the characters in the novel, ugly and distorted, dance around the sick man in a mad, fiendish circle. Rising from his hammock, Tony begins to plunge wildly through the jungle:

> At last he came into the open. The gates were open before him and trumpets were sounding along the walls, saluting his arrival; from bastion to bastion the message ran to the four points of the compass; petals of almond

and apple blossom were in the air; they carpeted the way as, after a summer storm, they lay in the orchards at Hetton. Gilded cupolas and spires of alabaster shone in the sunlight.

Ambrose announced, "The city is served."   [p. 221]

This city is indeed a transfigured Hetton, but it is stripped of all the sentimental drivel. Instead of ceilings groined and painted in diapers of red and gold and supported by shafts of polished granite with carved capitals, there are palm thatch roofs and breast-high walls of mud and wattle; instead of a society of vicious sophisticates presided over by a cruel and unfaithful wife, there is a community of savages ruled by a cunning lunatic. Tony's benefactor and, later, gaoler, Mr. Todd, has one great pleasure in life—having the works of Dickens read aloud to him. This innocent enjoyment is so great, in fact, that he imprisons his guest in the savannah and forces him to read again and again the collected works of that humane Victorian. Day after day, the readings testify to the ultimate victory of goodness and the sanctity of the personal dream—precisely those values which the hero's life-in-death refutes.[8] When Tony reaches *Great Expectations,* he must read about Wemmick, who, after a trying day in the jungles of the Inner Temple, can return to his miniature fortress, crank up the drawbridge, and drink tea with his aged parent. In England, Hetton is a silver-fox farm, Brenda has married Tony's best friend, and a certain interior decorator is thriving. Tony Last, literally imprisoned now in a literal wasteland, has nothing left of his dream but a heap of broken images. The fulfillment of Tony's humanism, his selfless devotion, his abnegation is an endless self-sacrifice enforced by a madman in the midst of a jungle. There is no City. Mrs. Beaver has covered it with chromium plating and converted it into flats.

In *Vile Bodies* Evelyn Waugh describes an airplane flight over England, taking Nina Blount and her obnoxious hus-

8. Alvin B. Kernan, "The Wall and the Jungle: The Early Novels of Evelyn Waugh," *Yale Review, 53* (1963), 219.

band Ginger Littlejohn to their honeymoon cottage with a nine-hole golf course in Monte Carlo. Ginger, waxing poetic, gazes at his native land and recalls some dimly remembered lines from a blue poetry book about "this scepter'd isle, this earth of majesty, this something or other Eden." Nina looks down from the plane and, sick to her stomach, sees not the England of the Renaissance but "a horizon of straggling red suburb; arterial roads dotted with little cars; factories, some of them working, others empty and decaying; a disused canal; some distant hills sown with bungalows; wireless masts and overhead power cables; men and women . . . indiscernible except as tiny spots" (p. 197).

Waugh, too, regards what was once "a precious stone set in the silver sea" and is obsessed with an overwhelming sense of loss. His laughter at the masses of dirty, moronic, corrupt, and fornicating beings beneath him cannot conceal his bitter rage. For the glory, the beauty, the dignity, and the grace of England have been destroyed, and Waugh, like Nina, sees only straggling red suburb, nauseating filth, and appalling decay.

2 GEORGE ORWELL

In George Orwell's *Coming Up for Air* (1939) a fat, aging insurance salesman named George Bowling decides to escape from the savagery and meanness of his dull middle-class existence and return to Lower Binfield, the unsullied rural town of his birth. Bowling can no longer tolerate the intricate web of jealousy, avarice, backbiting, and ugliness which is smothering his soul, but must breathe once again, if only for a moment, the clear, fresh air of a simpler era when even the poorest man could maintain a quiet dignity and the most consummate villain conceal a vein of humanity:

> You know the feeling I had. Coming up for air! Like the big sea turtles when they come paddling up to the surface, stick their noses out and fill their lungs with a great gulp before they sink down again among the seaweed and the octopuses.[1]

And so, fortified by a few pounds that he has managed to hide from his shrewish wife, Hilda, George Bowling sets out in search of his idyllic past. To his disgust and disillusionment, however, he discovers that Lower Binfield has become a growing industrial city complete with factories, munitions plants, choking chemical odors, polluted streams, lunatic asylums, noxious smells, nudist colonies, and endless miles of the "straggling red suburb" that Waugh despised. Instead of the leisurely, relaxed pace of life during his boyhood, George is rudely shoved and jostled by "the usual crowd that you can hardly fight your way through . . . streaming up the pavement, all of them with that insane fixed expression on their faces" (p. 29). Instead of rural quiet and serenity, bomber planes are continually flying overhead preparing for the approaching war. Wholesome, nourishing food has been replaced by "a sort of horrible soft stuff . . . oozing all over my tongue," and worse, people prefer the disgusting mess to the simple, hardy fare of the past. Everyone seems to have a ghastly cough, lice, scrofula, falling hair, loose dentures, and

1. George Orwell, *Coming Up for Air* (New York, 1939), p. 198.

bad breath. One by one, George's dreams and memories are shattered—a childhood sweetheart is now "a great, round-shouldered hag"; a hidden pool where George, as a boy, had seen huge carp is a rubbish dump; his father's corn and seed store has been ruthlessly absorbed by a large, impersonal chain; religious spirit has dwindled to the timid devotions of a few senile old men; his home has been converted into a cheap but pretentious tea shoppe. Infected by the filthy diseases of Progress, Modernity, and Industrialism, everything is now tawdry, debased, dirty. The precious past, with its values of human dignity, decency, and honesty, has been smothered by the irresistible weight of ignorance, viciousness, and ugliness. The truths cherished and preserved by generations of simple, hard-working, humble souls have been besmirched by the vileness of a new breed of streamlined men.

The past is dead, the present is intolerable, the future holds no promise of renewal. The future belongs to the sadists and the fanatics, to the criminally insane, who are fast gaining control over the world, to the mentally unbalanced, who know no morality or decency, to the blind, moronic masses whose life and meager thoughts are completely controlled by unscrupulous, power-crazed maniacs. On the second day of Bowling's stay in Lower Binfield, a British airplane on a training mission accidentally drops a bomb on the town:

> Afterwards (I got this out of the newspaper) the Air Ministry sent a chap to inspect the damage, and issued a report saying that the effects of the bomb were "disappointing." As a matter of fact it had only killed three people. [p. 265]

The macabre incident shocks George Bowling completely out of his dreams and illusions, and he sheepishly returns home to face the ceaseless nagging, burnt meals, and nasty complaints of Hilda, who is incapable of seeing anything but lewdness and infidelity in her husband's behavior.

Bowling has learned the bitter lesson that he can never come up for air, that he is condemned to live at the bottom of the foul, murky ocean of ignorance and brutality. It is not the meek who shall inherit the earth, but the streamlined men, the venal politicians, the unscrupulous crusaders. The once-meaningful distinctions between evil and good, tyranny and justice, fascist and anti-fascist are exposed as miserable shams, concealing the depravity and viciousness which ultimately obliterates all political and moral labels. Listening to the harangue of a "well-known anti-fascist," the ravings of a "human barrel-organ shooting propaganda at you," at a meeting of the Left Book Club, Bowling suddenly has a vision of what the speaker is actually seeing in his mind:

> It's a picture of himself smashing people's faces in with spanner. Fascist faces, of course. Smash! Right in the middle! The bones cave in like an eggshell and what was a face a minute ago is just a great big blob of strawberry jam. [p. 175]

It is this mindless, uncontrollable violence that has destroyed the values of Bowling's boyhood world and that heralds the future, for all rational opposition has been crippled by fear, senility, and moral blindness: "all the decent people are paralysed. Dead men and live gorillas. Doesn't seem to be anything between" (p. 189). Bowling has realized not only that he can never recover the past, but that the future will be even more horrid than the present:

> *It's all going to happen.* All the things you've got at the back of your mind, the things you're terrified of, the things that you tell yourself are just a nightmare or only happen in foreign countries. The bombs, the food-queues, the rubber truncheons, the barbed wire, the coloured shirts, the slogans, the enormous faces, the machine-guns squirting out of bedroom windows . . . There's no escape. [p. 267]

Coming Up for Air closes with this terrifying vision of war and its grim aftermath as the only certainties of human existence. World War II began three months after the novel was published.

George Orwell, like his character George Bowling, once believed that most human beings are decent chaps at heart and sought to recover the virtues of the past. Orwell believed that a regime based on the principles of democratic socialism could enable men to live a tolerable, even mildly pleasant life, and that such a regime could isolate and destroy the forces of violence, injustice, and tyranny. Like Bowling, Orwell went on a quixotic and fruitless quest for this decent life. He proclaimed himself a socialist, renounced his bourgeois background, lived for years as an impoverished member of the proletariat in the slums of Paris and London, fought in the Republican Army during the Spanish Civil War, and wrote in 1947 that "every line of serious work that I have written since 1936 has been for democratic socialism."[2] He championed the downtrodden masses, the common man, whom Orwell saw ruthlessly exploited by unscrupulous politicians and priests. All the complex ideological squabbles, the bitter feuds, the brief but violent skirmishes, the great wars themselves appeared to Orwell as aspects of the one simple question central to society: "Shall people . . . be allowed to live the decent, fully human life which is now technically achievable, or shan't they? Shall the common man be pushed back into the mud, or shall he not?"[3]

George Orwell longed all his life for the security and unambiguity of a neat, logical system, a clear set of rules and fixed standards with which he could order, classify, and arrange all men and institutions. He once speculated in a poem that:

> A happy vicar I might have been
> Two hundred years ago,
> To preach upon eternal doom
> And watch my walnuts grow.[4]

And indeed, it is just this sort of unshakable, even dull, religious certainty and intellectual repose that Orwell sought. But, to his profound unhappiness, Orwell grew up in a time when the values of the religious order were disintegrating,

2. Orwell, "Why I Write," *A Collection of Essays* (New York, 1954, Doubleday Anchor Book), p. 318.
3. Orwell, "Looking Back on the Spanish War," *Essays*, pp. 213–14.
4. Orwell, "Why I Write," *Essays*, p. 317.

and, unlike Evelyn Waugh, Christopher Hollis, and other talented writers, he was emotionally and intellectually unable to enter the cloister of the Catholic Church. The religious establishment seemed to Orwell merely another of "the smelly little orthodoxies which are now contending for our souls,"[5] a colossal fraud concealing the unbounded rapaciousness and lust for power of the priests. As a substitute for the no longer acceptable religious discipline, Orwell chose for a time revolutionary politics, democratic socialism, left-wing humanitarianism. Socialism—freed from the control of the crackpots, "humanized," and dedicated to the cause of justice, liberty, and the plight of the unemployed— seemed to Orwell the wonderfully logical, irrefutable solution for the horrors of "a world in which nobody is free, in which hardly anybody is secure, in which it is almost impossible to be honest and to remain alive":

> everyone who uses his brain knows that Socialism, as a world-system and wholeheartedly applied, is a way out. It would at least ensure our getting enough to eat . . . Socialism is such elementary common sense that I am sometimes amazed that it has not established itself already. The world is a raft sailing through space with, potentially, plenty of provisions for everybody; the idea that we must all co-operate and see to it that everyone does his fair share of the work and gets his fair share of the provisions, seems so blatantly obvious that one would say that no one could possibly fail to accept it unless he had some corrupt motive for clinging to the present system.[6]

The simplicity and lucidity of Orwell's vision is at once breathtaking and, as the author himself came to realize, hopelessly naïve. In the last years of his life, while never wholly renouncing socialism, Orwell learned that political problems are rarely simple and that the great social evils are never eliminated by the various panaceas of socialism,

5. Orwell, "Charles Dickens," *Essays*, p. 111.

6. Orwell, *The Road to Wigan Pier* (New York, Berkley, 1961), pp. 144–45.

communism, or enlightened capitalism. The injustice, lies, and poverty that he once viewed as the product of a few evil men and institutions now seemed to Orwell a bitter but inevitable portion of human existence. The hope of radical change and the victory of decency, the firm conviction that "the common man will win his fight sooner or later"[7] fades, in the last novels, into blackest pessimism and despair.

As David J. Dooley, in an article entitled "The Limitations of George Orwell," astutely observes, Orwell's acceptance of socialism as a comprehensive discipline and his adoption of a grossly simplified and abstracted view of society draws him into a series of irresolvable contradictions, forces him to play a peculiar game whose limitations compel him to hold mutually exclusive ideas as simultaneously true.[8] Thus Orwell, who all his life warned intellectuals of the dangers of slogans and meaningless catch-phrases, often falls into a sort of labeling game in which people are placed into various rigid categories, such as "stalinists," "anti-stalinists," "cryptos," "fascists," and "Blimps." Thus Orwell is able to rejoice that "religious belief . . . has largely vanished, dragging other kinds of nonsense with it"[9] and to lament that the "major problem of our time is the decay of the belief in personal immortality."[10] Thus Orwell declares himself a revolutionary socialist to the end of his life, even after he has written powerful and bitter exposés of the whole notion of progressive revolution and the socialist myth of history. David Dooley concludes that Orwell's "books are interesting, not as warnings of a prophet who realized the truth before anyone else, but as portraits of the mind of a man who . . . imprisoned himself inside the game he played."[11]

While it is necessary, as Dooley points out, to recognize the limitations of Orwell, one need not reject the works as nothing but the unconscious self-revelations of a psychologically disturbed individual. For the very quality in Orwell

7. Orwell, "Looking Back on the Spanish War," p. 214.
8. David J. Dooley, "The Limitations of George Orwell," *University of Toronto Quarterly, 28* (1958–59), 299.
9. Orwell, "Such, Such Were the Joys . . .," *Essays,* p. 51.
10. Orwell, "Looking Back on the Spanish War," p. 213.
11. "The Limitations of George Orwell," p. 299.

that Dooley criticizes is the source of the brilliance of the work and the fascination of his personality. At the center of Orwell's life and writings is the almost unbearable tension between the various societal games—with their rigid rules, strict codes, fixed values, and comprehensive principles—and the violent, often chaotic and soul-destroying revolt against these systems and games. Orwell's characters, like their author, long for order and quiet in a disordered, grotesque universe, but they are always unable to sink into the dull, secure world of ideology or indifference. Orwell's heroes are marked men, and if they do not have ugly facial birthmarks, like Flory in *Burmese Days,* they are cut off from the community of their fellow men by an inner, psychological birthmark. Orwell and his characters insist that their revolt is compulsive, actually against their will—in normal, moderately decent times, they tell us, they would have been perfectly content to be ministers or businessmen, quiet, responsible members of the establishment. It is the miserable and chaotic state of the world, evident to those with the barest measure of good taste and common sense, that drives them to rebellion. In "Why I Write" Orwell assures his readers that "In a peaceful age I might have written ornate or merely descriptive books, and might have remained unaware of my political loyalties. As it is I have been forced into becoming a sort of pamphleteer." And indeed, Orwell's personal history is a remarkable tale of a man who always seemed to be present at a scene or committed to an institution that was just beginning to collapse, to crumble, to dissolve into chaos. But the reader senses that Orwell would have been profoundly unhappy with the so-called solutions of any age; that despite his deeply felt need for the intellectual security of an ideology, he could not fall into complacency and acceptance because he was far too aware of, and revolted by, the hundreds of great and minuscule lies that all societies must continually tell themselves. Orwell's cross and his glory is precisely this inability to accept or condone even the most necessary human falsehoods.

Like most satirists, he continually assures his audience that his revolt against society is not motivated by perversity or arrogance, that in spite of all his good intentions to be a quiet, law-abiding citizen he is totally unable to conform to accepted behavior. In "Such, Such Were the Joys . . . ," an autobiographical record of his bitter experience at preparatory school, the author carefully traces this development of himself as unwilling rebel. Soon after his arrival at Crossgates, a snobbish, expensive boarding school, which accepted young Orwell as a scholarship student, the child reverts to bed-wetting, a catastrophe that first teaches him "the great, abiding lesson of my boyhood: that I was in a world where it was not possible for me to be good" (p. 13). The sensitive boy completely accepts the cruel judgment of the headmaster and his wife, known as Sim and Bingo, that bed-wetting is a "disgusting crime . . . for which the proper cure was a beating," but, in spite of his fervent prayers, he cannot avoid waking in the morning between clammy sheets. The canings he receives for his offenses seem perfectly reasonable to the child, for they are the logical concomitants of a harsh, unsympathetic world which cannot tolerate deviants of any kind. The boy's dilemma—the conflict between his immense longing to conform and the physical impossibility of conformity—is irresolvable, leaving him with a terrible sense of loneliness, isolation, and helplessness.

Orwell's brilliant account of his miserable life at Crossgates is the vehicle for a sweeping condemnation of the entire British system of education; yet, though the school is presented as an abominable prison, heavy with the nightmarish atmosphere of evil, injustice, and horror and run by two villains whose nastiness exceeds that of their models, Creakle and Fagan, the reader never questions the complete objectivity of the portrait. By repeatedly announcing his devotion to truth, by candidly admitting his own faults, by observing that the essay is written from the perspective of middle age, when his boyish terrors and prejudices have all faded, Orwell creates an aura of truth and integrity in his picture of Crossgates that obscures the large element of exaggeration, distortion, and sheer fantasy. The reader assumes that the children must indeed have been unbearably snobbish, the headmaster and his wife rotten social climbers and bullies, the facilities abominably filthy, the food disgusting, the discipline brutal, the education an unscrupulous sham. But Cyril Connolly, who was at school with Orwell, presents a radically different account of Crossgates (called St. Wulfric's) in *Enemies of Promise:*

> St. Wulfric's, where I went, was well run and vigorous, and did me good. We called the headmistress Flip and the headmaster Sambo. Flip, around whom the school revolved, was able, ambitious, temperamental, and energetic. She wanted it to be a success, to have more boys, to attract the sons of peers and to send them all to Eton . . . Sambo was a cold, business-like and dutiful consort. The morale of the school was high . . .[12]

It is difficult to believe that Crossgates and St. Wulfric's are the same school, yet Connolly and Orwell were close friends and share many of the same conclusions about the British school system. What distinguishes Orwell's frenzied, passionate evocation of Crossgates and Connolly's calm, humane, and rather dull recollection of prep school is not fundamental disagreement about the faults and merits of the school—they both speak of snobbery, spartan diet, cynical cramming for examinations, hypocritical "character building," unfair punishment, morbid sexual fears—but a profound difference in tone, atmosphere, and balance. *Enemies of Promise* is written by a calm individual who reviews his childhood from the detachment of middle age. In "Such, Such Were the Joys . . . ," on the other hand, the whole world seems out of proportion, distorted, grotesquely twisted by the author's feverish imagination. In "Why I Write," Orwell remarked that "one can write nothing readable unless one constantly struggles to efface one's personality" (p. 320), but it is precisely the shaping force of the author's personality, his peculiar vision, his perceptual idiosyncrasies which give the description of Crossgates school its power and significance. In fact, "Such, Such Were the Joys . . ." is wonderfully readable and immensely effective *because* of Orwell's inability to efface his own personality.

12. Cyril Connolly, *Enemies of Promise* (London, 1938), pp. 206–07.

In an essay on Charles Dickens, Orwell astutely praises Dickens for his marvelous "power of entering into the child's point of view," his remarkable ability "to stand both inside and outside the child's mind in such a way that the same scene can be wild burlesque or sinister reality,"[13] and it is this same quality which characterizes "Such, Such Were the Joys . . ." For, at the same time that the mature Orwell is discussing the many changes wrought by the thirty years that have elapsed since his prep school days, he is present as a young child, smarting under the blows of the cruel Sim, suffering from the snobbery of his fellow students, desperately trying to please Bingo, secretly hating school and God and himself. Orwell's account of Crossgates and his attack on the British schools is far more meaningful and impressive than Cyril Connolly's similar account, because where Connolly relates a few amusing anecdotes and makes some interesting generalizations, Orwell recreates an entire world, reproduces in detail the child's own vision, fills the reader with the boy's sense of disgust and outrage.

Above all, Orwell captures the child's sense of physical revulsion. The pampered snobs who torment the lonely child are made uncomfortably real in the description of a little fair-haired lord who "had a choking fit at dinner, and a stream of snot ran out of his nose onto his plate in a way horrible to see" (p. 15). Adults are grotesque monsters of enormous size, with "their ungainly, rigid bodies, their coarse wrinkled skins, their great relaxed eyelids, their yellow teeth, and the whiffs of musty clothes and beer and sweat and tobacco that disengage from them at every moment" (p. 52). And the wretched, overcrowded, dirty life at Crossgates is pictured in a great mass of revolting details eminently worthy of Dean Swift. "One seems always to be walking the tightrope over a cesspool," Orwell writes, and indeed, his balance is far from steady:

> there were the pewter bowls out of which we had our porridge. They had overhanging rims, and under the rims there were accumulations of sour porridge, which

13. Orwell, "Charles Dickens," p. 67.

could be flaked off in long strips. The porridge itself, too, contained more lumps, hairs and unexplained black things than one would have thought possible, unless someone were putting them there on purpose . . . And there was the slimy water of the plunge bath . . . and the always-damp towels with their cheesy smell; and, on occasional visits in the winter, the murky sea-water of the local Baths . . . on which I once saw floating a human turd. And the sweaty smell of the changing-room with its greasy basins, and giving on this, the row of filthy, dilapidated lavatories . . . It is not easy for me to think of my schooldays without seeming to breathe in a whiff of something cold and evil-smelling—a sort of compound of sweaty stockings, dirty towels, faecal smells blowing along corridors, forks with old food between the prongs, neck-of-mutton stew, and the banging doors of the lavatories and the echoing chamber-pots in the dormitories.

[pp. 29–30]

This incredible preoccupation with "the W.C. and dirty handkerchief side of life," with the sheer physical horror of existence, is the signature of all of Orwell's work and has led outraged critics like Anthony West to speculate on the author's "psychic wound"[14] or the perils of a hyperdeveloped sense of smell. But the catalogue of filthy details serves a crucial artistic purpose in Orwell's writings, for like Waugh's shocking cruelty and audacity, it creates the turbulent atmosphere of a mad world, the sense of a grotesque, twisted universe, the nausea and despair of being entrapped in a diseased society. Orwell's claim that good prose must be "like a window pane" through which one sees clearly into reality is simply a rhetorical device intended to induce the reader into a state of easy credulity and the suspension of disbelief. Isaac Rosenfeld, in *An Age of Enormity,* sums up a great deal of Orwell criticism when he insists that "Orwell was fair, honest, unassuming, and reliable in everything he wrote."[15] Orwell's "honesty," however, is not that of a detached ob-

14. Anthony West, quoted in Dooley, p. 292.
15. Isaac Rosenfeld, *An Age of Enormity* (Cleveland, 1943), p. 251.

server but that of a writer who is passionately involved in
and revolted by the world he is attacking; his technique is
not the impartial recording of all the facts but the clever
and often malicious editing of experience, so that, for example, the filthy occurrences of six years of prep school seem
like the everyday experience of the child.

The bitter conflict in the schoolboy's mind between the
acceptance of the codes of his society and the inability to
live up to them is intensified in Orwell's next experience—
serving with the Indian Imperial Police in Burma. In the
light of the progressive, libertarian beliefs expressed in most
of his works, it seems truly incredible that Orwell should
have found himself in his early twenties in the employ of the
British Raj, but one must not underestimate the "Kipling-
esque side to his character which made him romanticise the
Raj and its mystique."[16] Christopher Hollis met Orwell in
Rangoon in 1925 and recalls their conversation:

> We had a long talk and argument. In the side of him
> which he revealed to me at that time there was no trace
> of liberal opinions. He was at pains to be the imperial
> policeman, explaining that the theories of no punish-
> ment and no beating were all very well at public schools
> but that they did not work with the Burmese—in fact
> that
>
> > Libbaty's a kind o' thing
> > Thet don't agree with niggers.[17]

That the great humanitarian and socialist, the man described
by V. S. Pritchett as "a kind of a saint and the wintry con-
science of a whole generation,"[18] should have held such a
view must have been terribly painful, in retrospect, to Orwell, and, indeed, he writes of his experience in Burma in
The Road to Wigan Pier: "For five years I had been part of
an oppressive system, and it had left me with a bad con-

16. Malcolm Muggeridge, quoted in Christopher Hollis, *George Orwell* (Chicago, 1956), p. 28.

17. Christopher Hollis, *George Orwell* (Chicago, 1956), p. 27.

18. V. S. Pritchett, quoted in Dooley, p. 291.

science . . . I was conscious of an immense weight of guilt that I had got to expiate."[19] Part of this expiation was the writing of his first novel, *Burmese Days*, published in 1934.

In "Why I Write," Orwell describes *Burmese Days* as one of a species of "enormous naturalistic novels with unhappy endings, full of detailed descriptions and arresting similes, and also full of purple passages in which words were used partly for the sake of their sound" (p. 315). As an "enormous naturalistic novel" *Burmese Days* is a failure. The unhappy love story that is the focal point of the novel's meager plot is uninteresting and amateurish. John Flory, a lonely English timber merchant in Burma, cursed with a hideous, jagged birthmark on his cheek, falls in love with Elizabeth, a spiritually and mentally empty, coarse, and revolting young woman who has come east to find a husband. Various natural and unnatural causes (including a small earthquake) conspire to prevent Flory from proposing marriage, and, when finally he is disgraced before the English community and Elizabeth by his Burmese mistress, he shoots himself through the heart. Behind this clumsy apparatus, however, there is a bitter satire on the British Raj and a fascinating portrait of the struggle in Orwell between the powerful temptation to conform and the compulsive need to rebel.

Sir Richard Rees, in *George Orwell: Fugitive from the Camp of Victory*, complains that the mood of *Burmese Days* is "atrabilious," for Orwell cannot abide either side—"The British are hysterical and the Burmese are childish and corrupt."[20] And indeed, if read from the standard liberal approach to imperialism—an oppressive and tyrannical force that crushes the weak and defenseless natives—Orwell's first novel seems misguided and riddled with internal conflict. For Orwell's criticism of the Raj is not that it deprived the innocent natives of the self-government they deserved but that it was morally, spiritually, and physically degrading for both ruler and ruled, bringing out the worst element in both. Orwell is hardly a champion of the downtrodden Bur-

19. *The Road to Wigan Pier,* p. 127.
20. Richard Rees, *George Orwell: Fugitive from the Camp of Victory* (Carbondale, 1961), p. 28.

mese people, for while he despised the Imperial Police and the whole oppressive system it stood for, he was constantly enraged by the "evil-spirited little beasts who tried to make my job impossible."[21] In the essay "Shooting an Elephant," Orwell remarks that, though he looked on the British Raj as despicable, he felt that "the greatest joy in the world would be to drive a bayonet into a Buddhist priest's guts" (p. 155). In his treatment of imperialism, Orwell, the radical socialist, comes remarkably close in principle, if not in spirit, to Evelyn Waugh, the archconservative, for like Waugh, Orwell insists that the White Man's Burden is a ridiculous sham, concealing cynical self-interest, sadism, lunacy, and incredible stupidity in both the colonialists and the natives. But Orwell could not laugh cruelly and maliciously like the author of *Black Mischief* at the posturings and idiocies of the supporters of the Empire. Haunted by "Innumerable remembered faces—faces of prisoners in the dock, of men waiting in the condemned cells, of subordinates I had bullied and aged peasants I had snubbed, of servants and coolies I had hit with my fist in moments of rage,"[22] Orwell had to rail violently against the "stifling, stultifying world" in which he had lived.

Burmese Days is an attempt to portray a society without hope or meaning or lasting pleasure, a community bereft of values and of justification for its existence, a world where communication, healthy sexual relations, happiness have been destroyed. As in "Such, Such Were the Joys . . .," the sheer weight of ugliness, filth, and vileness is overwhelming. With the exception, perhaps, of the hero, all the persons in the novel are caricatures, distorted and ludicrous images of varieties of human evil, folly, and perversion. There is Verral, the surly snob whose only gods were "horsemanship and physical fitness" and who "despised the entire non-military population of India, a few famous polo players excepted"; Ellis, the vicious paranoiac, who regrets that the English are not allowed to kill natives indiscriminately; Lackerseen, who turns to alcoholism and wild orgies as an escape from his

21. Orwell, "Shooting an Elephant," *Essays*, p. 155.
22. *The Road to Wigan Pier*, p. 127.

shrewish wife; Dr. Veriswami, the well-meaning but idiotic Madrasi Brahmin, who fanatically worships British Culture long after it has proven its sterility; and, a truly brilliant creation, U Po Kyin, the immensely fat and diabolically cunning civil servant, whose machinations to be elected a member of the all-white European club ultimately determine the fate of the entire British colony. In the satirical portrait of this last character, Orwell concentrates all of his fascinated interest in and virulent hatred of the Burmese:

> Unblinking, rather like a great porcelain idol, U Po Kyin gazed out into the fierce sunlight. He was a man of fifty, so fat that for years he had not risen from his chair without help, and yet shapely and even beautiful in his grossness; for the Burmese do not sag and bulge like white men, but grow fat symmetrically, like fruits swelling . . . He was swollen with the bodies of his enemies: a thought from which he extracted something very near poetry.[23]

U Po Kyin's pervasive function in the plot—he subtly controls the lives of all the characters in the novel—is an assertion of a point Orwell made in "Shooting an Elephant," that "when the white man turns tyrant it is his own freedom he destroys" (p. 159). The rather comic Subdivisional Magistrate of Kyauktada with his obesity, his yellow skin, and his great numbers of small, perfect teeth, stained red by betel juice and the blood of his victims, actually commands more power than the great Imperial Police of Burma.

An even more memorable, impressive, and significant force in *Burmese Days* than U Po Kyin, however, is the scene itself, with its strange blended qualities of decay, ugliness, riot, and immense beauty. In *The Road to Wigan Pier* Orwell remarks that "the landscapes of Burma, which, when I was among them, so appalled me as to assume the qualities of nightmare, afterward stayed so hauntingly in my mind that I was obliged to write a novel about them to get rid of them." Like Waugh's jungle, Orwell's landscapes are more

23. Orwell, *Burmese Days* (New York, 1934), p. 1.

symbolic than literal, expressing all the grotesqueness, cruelty, and disintegration of the characters and the British Raj itself:

> By the roadside, just before you got to the jail, the fragments of a stone pagoda were littered, cracked and overthrown by the strong roots of a peepul tree. The angry carved faces of demons looked up from the grass where they had fallen. Nearby another peepul tree had turned itself round a palm, uprooting it and bending it backwards in a wrestle that had lasted a decade.   [p. 125]

Beyond the ruined temple there was a cemetery: "The creeping jasmine, with tiny orange-hearted flowers, had overgrown everything. Among the jasmine, large rat-holes led down into the graves" (p. 239). And dominating the entire scene are the ever-watchful vultures, waiting patiently in the dung-whitened branches of the big pyinkado trees for the violence and bloodshed that will one day sweep over Burma.

John Flory, the main character of *Burmese Days,* is the archetypal Orwellian hero. He is a marked man, literally and figuratively, for the "hideous birthmark stretching in a ragged crescent down his left cheek, from the eye to the corner of his chin" symbolizes his unwilling alienation from society. Flory is an outcast, a man branded with the mark of Cain because of his inability to accept the standards of the community. Rejected by society, he sets himself up as its critic and bitterly attacks its fundamental values, declaring to Dr. Veriswami that "before we've finished we'll have wrecked the whole Burmese national culture . . . We're not civilizing them, we're only rubbing our dirt on to them . . . I see (the Englishman) as a kind of up-to-date, hygienic, self-satisfied louse. Creeping round the world building prisons. They build a prison and call it progress" (p. 42).

Flory expresses many of Orwell's own views on the Empire, but in the very act of denouncing the British Raj, he exposes the basic weakness of his character and the internally corrupting effect of his venomous existence. What begins as righteous indignation gradually becomes little more than the ceaseless carping of a sick man. The nobility of Flory's views is continually undermined by his lack of sympathy for other human beings, his cynicism, his almost paranoiac exaggeration of the evils around him, his tendency to make wild statements, like "The British Empire is simply a device for giving trade monopolies to the English—or rather to gangs of Jews and Scotchmen" (p. 40). Even more degrading is Flory's unwillingness to stand up publicly for the values he professes, in private, to believe in. In spite of his constant denunciations of the rottenness of the society around him, he is more imprisoned in the twisted mores and vicious lies of the corrupt world in which he lives than any of the characters of the novel. Flory clearly perceives the vileness of his life in Burma, but he cannot bear the disapproval of those he claims to hate. Thus he is driven to betray his few friends, his beliefs, and, finally, himself. He takes his life not in an act of defiance or in despair of the world but because he has been disgraced before the petty, vicious fools he despised, in the church he had viewed as the symbol of alien beliefs destroying native culture. His birthmark is a symbol not of defiant resistance but of a terrible, fatal sickness of soul. If Flory, then, is indeed a thinly disguised picture of George Orwell himself, *Burmese Days* is deeply colored by the author's self-hatred, for Flory's moral cowardice, his spiritual weakness, his filthy existence make him a wholly unsavory and unheroic hero.

The bitter self-disgust displayed in *Burmese Days* and recalled in "Such, Such Were the Joys . . ." ("I had no money, I was weak, I was ugly, I was unpopular, I had a chronic cough, I was cowardly, I smelt") receives its fullest expression in Orwell's second novel, where it actually overwhelms the whole book. While John Flory was rather weak and pitiful, Gordon Comstock, the "hero" of *Keep the Aspidistra Flying* (1936) is obnoxious and detestable. Comstock, a young, self-styled poet, revolts self-consciously against the world of the money god and wage slave by quitting a well-paying job at an advertising agency and falling into a bohemian existence on the fringes of society. This parallels Orwell's own decision, upon returning to England from Burma, to live as a *plongeur* (dishwasher) in Paris and as a tramp in London. But Orwell's appraisal of his character's revolt, so much like his own, is far from sympathetic, for, as Gordon Comstock sinks deeper and deeper into poverty, his carping criticisms of the middle class sound increasingly shrill and grating, he seems increasingly unresponsive to human love and kindness, his cynicism, stupidity, and pride become intolerable. Under the sheer weight of Gordon's ugliness, the novel's supposed message—that the corrosive power of money has become the supreme force in society—is smothered and forgotten. In *Burmese Days* Orwell managed to sustain a delicate balance between satirical attack on the British rule and satirical attack on the revolt against British rule. The two elements, rather than canceling each other out, worked to reveal each other's viciousness and depravity. But this balance is not maintained in *Keep the Aspidistra Flying*, for Gordon Comstock's rebellion becomes so offensive that when, at the end of the novel, he finally gives in to the pressure of society and moves into the narrow middle-class world that had been waiting for him, the reader is deeply relieved, even gratified.

Keep the Aspidistra Flying was, quaintly enough, banned in Australia,[24] no doubt for its comment on contraception and premarital intercourse. For it is only when his girl friend, Rosemary, has announced to him that she is pregnant that Gordon is restored to a sort of feeble sanity and decides to return to a moderately human existence. Comstock rejects the philosophy of contraception, because it is the money god, he claims, who created sexual restraints and who "lays the sleek, estranging shield between the lover and his bride." If the Australian censors, however, believed that *Keep the Aspidistra Flying* could titillate anyone, they had very deep faith in the prurience of the average reader, for it is an essential condition of all of Orwell's novels that love is impossible and that sexual intercourse is rather dirty and unpleasant. When Gordon and Rosemary finally do have intercourse (without contraceptive), it is not in the pleasant countryside

24. Hollis, p. 69.

where "the warm light poured over them as though a membrane across the sky had broken,"[25] but in Gordon's dark and verminous garret. The scene could not be less romantic or exciting:

> "This isn't wise," he said.
> "I don't care. I wish I'd done it years ago."
> "We'd much better not."
> "Yes."
> "No."
> "Yes!"
> After all, she was too much for him. He had wanted her so long, and he could not stop to weigh the consequences. So it was done at last, without much pleasure, on Mother Meakin's dingy bed. Presently Rosemary got up and rearranged her clothes. The room, though stuffy, was dreadfully cold . . . She felt dismayed, disappointed, and very cold.   [p. 221]

Orwell cannot accept love as a viable alternative to human suffering and loneliness. Flory, in *Burmese Days,* adores a disgusting and spiritually empty girl who rejects him; George Bowling, in *Coming Up for Air,* is married to a shrew who makes his life miserable; Winston Smith, in *1984,* "loves" only a political revolt against the Party; Gordon Comstock in *Keep the Aspidistra Flying,* can only understand love of money. Each character believes that society, or the twentieth century, or capitalism, or the State has robbed love of its meaning and value, but the aggregate of failure clearly places the responsibility on fundamental flaws in man himself.

Keep the Aspidistra Flying is prefaced by an adapted quotation from I Corinthians 13, in which Orwell substitutes "money" for St. Paul's "charity." Thus, "Money suffereth long, and is kind; money envieth not; money vaunteth not itself, is not puffed up, doth not behave unseemly . . . And now abideth faith, hope and money, but the greatest of these is money," etc. Presumably, then, the book will be about the replacement of religious values by the money cult, but this

25. Orwell, *Keep the Aspidistra Flying* (New York, 1936), p. 139.

55

purpose is never realized. Instead, the novel is a prolonged attack on those who feel compelled, in their revolt against middle-class values, to substitute money for every other motive and to distort the entire world to fit their own rebellion. Rather than a demonstration of the corrupting effect of the money code on society, Orwell presents the corrosive effect of rebellion on the individual—indeed on himself. *Keep the Aspidistra Flying* is not simply a work of self-deprecation, however; it is a bitter satire on the satirist, on the intellectual and emotional deterioration inevitably brought on by intense, unremitting hatred and by preoccupation with evil. Gordon Comstock succeeds only in besmirching himself with the dirt he wished to fling at the money god. He fulfills, even surpasses, the popular image of the satirist—narrow-minded, irritable, intolerant, ignorant, vain, arrogant—and his rejection of life arises not out of a noble quest for lost values but out of his personal frustrations and deficiencies. Gordon, as satirist, is a "hard-attacker" whose role is wholly destructive; he not only predicts the coming war, he looks forward to it eagerly:

> Our civilization is dying. It *must* be dying. But it isn't going to die in its bed. Presently the aeroplanes are coming. Zoom-whizz-crash! The western world going up in a roar of high explosives. . . . It was a sound which, at that moment, he ardently desired to hear.   [p. 21]

This satirist knows no compromises, no middle ground, no moderation, no restraint—he can only conceive of complete revolt or complete capitulation. When Gordon rejects the money god, he wishes to sink underground, "down in the safe, soft womb of the earth, where there is no getting of jobs or losing of jobs, no relatives or friends to plague you, no hope, fear, ambition, honour, duty—no *duns* of any kind" (p. 203). When the revolt fails, he turns to abject money worship. Tom Hopkinson, in his essay *George Orwell*, claims that *Keep the Aspidistra Flying* ends on a "positive note: . . . Rosemary is about to have a baby, the couple decide to marry, and Comstock discovers the middle-class pleasures of owning some furniture and a place to put it, and the middle-class virtues of paying one's way, building up a family and putting the best face on life one can."[26] But Gordon's insistence, on his wedding day, upon at once buying an aspidistra for the newlyweds' apartment is a symbol not of his recognition of the necessity of making enough money to support a family but of his total surrender to all the mean, petty, degrading values that Orwell sees in the money code. *Keep the Aspidistra Flying* is a failure as a satire on middle-class morality, but it is an extraordinary success at representing the satirist as a repulsive, intolerable fool, whose revolt is hopeless.

In "Such, Such Were the Joys . . ." Orwell exposed the myth of the English public school; in *Burmese Days* he attacked the myth of the British Raj; in two short journals of the 1930s—*Down and Out in Paris and London* (1933) and *The Road to Wigan Pier* (1937)—he chronicled the breakdown of the myth of capitalism. The latter documents are not technically satires, for they propose merely to record Orwell's own experience during the depression years, and their merits presumably lie in the author's renowned "honesty" and in his clear, concise prose style. But in choosing his details, in ordering his experience, Orwell employed all the devices he later used in *Animal Farm* and *1984*. Orwell's prose is never the simple, colorless "window pane" he claims as his ideal; rather it always involves what Northrop Frye calls "the mythical patterns of experience, the attempts to give form to the shifting ambiguities and complexities of unidealized existence."[27] The satirist takes the vast mass of empirical data and, consciously or unconsciously, selects those details, almost always grotesque and ugly, which justify his attitude toward experience. As Frye observes, "The satirist has to select his absurdities, and the act of selection is a moral act."[28] One might add a creative act as well, for it

26. Tom Hopkinson, *George Orwell* (London, 1953), p. 21.
27. Northrop Frye, *Anatomy of Criticism* (Princeton, 1957), p. 223.
28. Frye, p. 224.

is in the organizing, arranging, and shaping of his material that the satirist's art is revealed. Satirical prose, then, is not a transparent medium through which the reader is given a view of reality, but a very peculiar lens, which renders distorted and often grotesque images of society. In *Down and Out in Paris and London,* for example, Orwell's experience in the world of the drunks, beggars, tramps, thieves, and prostitutes who live on the fringes of "civilized" society is seen as a descent into a seething, squalid inferno, a fantasy world where all is ugliness, noise, decay, rot, collapse: "It was a very narrow street—a ravine of tall, leprous houses, lurching towards one another in queer attitudes, as though they had all been frozen in the act of collapse."[29]

Even when Orwell asserts that his prose is devoid of satiric intent, his work assumes the forms of ironic fantasy or myth, not of realism. In the spirit of a scientist observing the behavior of a peculiar species of rodent, Orwell "relates" in *Down and Out* a grotesquely comical story told by Charlie, "one of the local curiosities." The tale is vicious and sadistic, permeated with demonic imagery and an atmosphere of horror which the ironic humor only heightens. Charlie, a debauched youth, cruelly rapes a peasant girl whose parents had sold her into slavery. In the few moments of violent lust in a cellar flooded with a garish red glare, "a heavy, stifling red, as though the light were shining through bowls of blood," Charlie asserts that "I captured the supreme happiness, the highest and most refined emotion to which human beings can attain . . . That is Love. That was the happiest day of my life" (pp. 11–12). Orwell is careful to point out three times that Charlie "was a youth of family and education," and the tale is most clearly a satire exposing the sexual cruelty that lurks beneath middle-class morality. But Orwell denies all ironic purpose, concluding blandly, "He was a curious specimen, Charlie. I describe him, just to show what diverse characters could be found flourishing in the Coq d'Or quarter" (p. 12).

The demonic imagery is even more apparent in Orwell's

29. Orwell, *Down and Out in Paris and London* (New York, Berkley, 1959), p. 5.

superb description of his life as a *plongeur* in the subbase-
ments of a huge Parisian hotel:

> The kitchen was like nothing I had ever seen or imag-
> ined—a stifling, low-ceilinged inferno of a cellar, red lit
> from the fires, and deafening with oaths and the clang-
> ing of pots and pans . . . The chargings to and fro in the
> narrow passages, the collisions, the yells, the struggling
> with crates and trays and blocks of ice, the heat, the
> darkness, the furious festering quarrels which there was
> no time to fight out—they pass description.   [p. 48]

Clearly Orwell is going beyond straight realism and is creating, in the description of a plongeur's life, as he does later
with the miner's existence in *The Road to Wigan Pier,* an
image of a modern hell and a sweeping condemnation of
capitalism. Orwell's brilliant, imaginative descriptions stand,
in their great power, as an eloquent justification of the art
of satire, for the heavy didacticism of many of Orwell's essays
is overwhelmed by the force of his mythic descriptions:

> All round was the lunar landscape of slag-heaps, and to
> the north, through the passes, as it were, between the
> mountains of slag, you could see the factory chimneys
> sending out their plumes of smoke. The canal path was
> a mixture of cinders and frozen mud, criss-crossed by
> the imprints of innumerable clogs, and all round, as far
> as the slag-heaps in the distance, stretched . . . pools of
> stagnant water. . . . It seemed a world from which vege-
> tation had been banished; nothing existed except smoke,
> shale, ice, mud, ashes and foul water.   [*Wigan,* p. 96]

The true vehicle, then, for Orwell's bitter condemnation of
capitalism is not the pseudo-philosophical essay but the
satirical description, the world seen as a grotesque charnel
house, stifling hot or horribly cold, reeking with the obscene
stench of human sweat and excrement, choked with filth and
the ashes of a dead civilization.

Throughout Orwell's early novels, journals, and essays,
democratic socialism existed as a sustaining vision that kept

the author from total despair of the human condition, but Orwell's bitter experience in the Spanish Civil War and the shock of the Nazi–Soviet pact signaled the breakdown of this last hope and the beginning of the mental and emotional state out of which grew *Animal Farm* and *1984*. The political disappointments of the late '30s and '40s did not in themselves, however, disillusion Orwell—they simply brought to the surface themes and tensions present in his work from the beginning. As we observed earlier, the socialism Orwell believed in was not a hardheaded, "realistic" approach to society and politics but a rather sentimental, utopian vision of the world as a "raft sailing through space, with, potentially, plenty of provisions for everybody," provided men, who, after all, are basically decent, would simply use common sense and not be greedy. Such naïve beliefs could only survive while Orwell was preoccupied with his attacks on the British Raj, the artist in society, or the capitalist system. The moment events compelled him to turn his critical eye on the myth of socialism and the "dictatorship of the proletariat," he discerned fundamental lies and corruption. Orwell, in his last years, was a man who experienced daily the disintegration of the beliefs of a lifetime, who watched in horror while his entire life work was robbed of meaning.

The first of his great cries of despair was *Animal Farm* (1946), a satirical beast fable which, curiously enough, has been heralded as Orwell's lightest, gayest work. Laurence Brander, in his biography of Orwell, paints a charming but wholly inaccurate picture of *Animal Farm*, presenting it as "one of those apparently chance pieces a prose writer throws off . . . a sport out of his usual way," supposedly written by Orwell in a state where "the gaiety in his nature had completely taken charge . . . writing about animals, whom he loved."[30] The surface gaiety, the seeming good humor and casualness, the light, bantering tone are, of course, part of the convention of beast fables, and *Animal Farm* would be a very bad tale indeed if it did not employ these devices. But it is a remarkable achievement precisely because Orwell uses the apparently frivolous form of the animal tale to convey

30. Laurence Brander, *George Orwell* (London, 1954), p. 171.

with immense power his profoundly bitter message. Critics like Laurence Brander and Tom Hopkinson who marvel at Orwell's "admirable good humour and detachment"[31] miss, I think, the whole point of the piece they praise. *Animal Farm* does indeed contain much gaiety and humor, but even in the most comic moments there is a disturbing element of cruelty or fear that taints the reader's hearty laughter. While Snowball, one of the leaders of the revolution of farm animals against their master, is organizing "the Egg Production Committee for the hens, the Clean Tails League for the cows, the Wild Comrades' Re-education Committee . . . , the Whiter Wool Movement for the sheep," Napoleon the sinister pig tyrant, is carefully educating the dogs for his own evil purposes. Similarly, the "confessions" forced from the animals in Napoleon's great purges are very funny, but when the dogs tear the throats out of the "guilty" parties and leave a pile of corpses at the tyrant's feet, the scene ceases to amuse. Orwell's technique is similar to the device we have seen in Waugh, who relates ghastly events in a comic setting.

Another critical mistake in appraising *Animal Farm* is made, I believe, by critics like Christopher Hollis who talk of the overriding importance of the author's love of animals[32] and fail to understand that Orwell in *Animal Farm* loves animals only as much or as little as he loves human beings. To claim that he hates the pigs because they represent human tyrants and sympathizes with the horses because they are dumb animals is absurd. Nor is it necessary, as Hollis believes, that the truly successful animal fable carry with it "a gay and light-hearted message."[33] Indeed, the very idea of representing human traits in animals is rather pessimistic. What is essential to the success of the satirical beast fable, as Ellen Douglass Leyburn observes, is the author's "power to keep his reader conscious simultaneously of the human traits satirized and of the animals as animals."[34] The storyteller

31. Hopkinson, p. 31.
32. Hollis, p. 148.
33. Ibid., p. 147.
34. Ellen Douglass Leyburn, "Animal Stories," in *Modern Satire,* ed. Alvin Kernan (New York, 1962), p. 215.

61

must never allow the animals to be simply beasts, in which case the piece becomes a nonsatirical children's story, or to be merely transparent symbols, in which case the piece becomes a dull sermon. Orwell proved, in *Animal Farm,* his remarkable ability to maintain this delicate, satiric balance.

The beast fable, an ancient satiric technique in which the characteristic poses of human vice and folly are embodied in animals, is, as Kernan points out, "an unrealistic, expressionistic device"[35] which stands in bold contrast with Orwell's previous realistic manner. But the seeds for *Animal Farm* are present in the earlier works, not only in the metaphors likening men to beasts but, more important, in Orwell's whole attitude toward society, which he sees as an aggregation of certain classes or types. The types change somewhat in appearance according to the setting—from the snobbish pukka sahibs, corrupt officials, and miserable natives of *Burmese Days* to the obnoxious nouveaux riches, greedy restaurateurs, and overworked plongeurs of *Down and Out in Paris and London,* but there remains the basic notion that men naturally divide themselves into a limited number of groups, which can be isolated and characterized by the astute observer. This notion is given dramatic reality in *Animal Farm,* where societal types are presented in the various kinds of farm animals—pigs for exploiters, horses for laborers, dogs for police, sheep for blind followers, etc. The beast fable need not convey an optimistic moral, but it cannot portray complex individuals, and thus it can never sustain the burden of tragedy. The characters of a satirical animal story may be sly, vicious, cynical, pathetic, lovable, or intelligent, but they can only be seen as members of large social groups and not as individuals.

Animal Farm has been interpreted most frequently as a clever satire on the betrayal of the Russian Revolution and the rise of Stalin. Richard Rees comments that "the struggle of the farm animals, having driven out their human exploiter, to create a free and equal community takes the form of a most ingeniously worked-out recapitulation of the history

---

35. "Introduction to Orwell's *Animal Farm,*" in *Modern Satire,* p. 106.

of Soviet Russia from 1917 up to the Teheran Conference."[36]
And indeed, despite Soviet critics who claim to see only a
general satire on bureaucracy in *Animal Farm*,[37] the political allegory is inevitable. Inspired by the prophetic death-
bed vision of Old Major, a prize Middle White boar, the
maltreated animals of Manor Farm successfully revolt against
Mr. Jones, their bad farmer, and found their own utopian
community, Animal Farm. The control of the revolution
falls naturally upon the pigs, particularly upon Napoleon,
"a large, rather fierce-looking Berkshire boar, not much of
a talker, but with a reputation for getting his own way," and
on Snowball, "a more vivacious pig than Napoleon, quicker
in speech and more inventive, but . . . not considered to have
the same depth of character." Under their clever leadership
and with the help of the indefatigable cart horses Boxer and
Clover, the animals manage to repulse the attacks of their
rapacious human neighbors, Mr. Pilkington and Mr. Frederick. With the farm secured from invasion and the Seven
Commandments of Animalism painted on the end wall of
the big barn, the revolution seems complete; but as the
community develops, it is plain that there are graver dangers
than invasion. The pigs at once decide that milk and apples
are essential to their well being. Squealer, Napoleon's lieu-
tenant and the ablest talker, explains the appropriation:

> "Comrades!" he cried. "You do not imagine, I hope, that
> we pigs are doing this in a spirit of selfishness and privi-
> lege? Many of us actually dislike milk and apples . . .
> Our sole object in taking these things is to preserve our
> health. Milk and apples (this has been proven by Science,
> comrades) contain substances absolutely necessary to the
> well-being of a pig . . . We pigs are brainworkers . . .
> Day and night we are watching over your welfare. It is
> for *your* sake that we drink that milk and eat those
> apples. Do you know what would happen if we pigs
> failed in our duty? Jones would come back!"[38]

36. Rees, *George Orwell*, p. 84.
37. Hollis, p. 145.
38. Orwell, *Animal Farm* (New York, 1946), p. 30.

A growing rivalry between Snowball and Napoleon is decisively decided by Napoleon's vicious hounds, who drive Snowball off the farm. Laurence Brander sees Snowball as a symbol of "altruism, the essential social virtue" and his expulsion as the defeat of "his altruistic laws for giving warmth, food and comfort to all the animals."[39] This is very touching, but unfortunately there is no indication that Snowball is any less corrupt or power-mad than Napoleon. Indeed, it is remarked, concerning the appropriation of the milk and apples, that "All the pigs were in full agreement on this point, even Snowball and Napoleon" (p. 30). The remainder of *Animal Farm* is a chronicle of the consolidation of Napoleon's power through clever politics, propaganda, and terror. Dissenters are ruthlessly murdered, and when Boxer can no longer work, he is sold to the knacker. One by one, the Commandments of Animalism are perverted or eliminated, until all that is left is:

ALL ANIMALS ARE EQUAL
BUT SOME ANIMALS ARE MORE EQUAL THAN OTHERS.

After that, it does not seem strange when the pigs live in Jones' house, walk on two legs, carry whips, wear human clothes, take out subscriptions to *John Bull, Tit-Bits,* and the *Daily Mirror,* and invite their human neighbors over for a friendly game of cards. The game ends in a violent argument when Napoleon and Pilkington play an ace of spades simultaneously, but for the animals there is no real quarrel. "The creatures outside looked from pig to man, and from man to pig, and from pig to man again; but already it was impossible to say which was which."

The interpretation of *Animal Farm* in terms of Soviet history (Major, Napoleon, Snowball represent Lenin, Stalin, Trotsky) has been made many times[40] and shall not be pursued further here. It is amusing, however, that many of the Western critics who astutely observe the barbs aimed at Russia fail completely to grasp Orwell's judgment of the

39. Brander, p. 175.
40. E.g. Hollis, p. 145.

West. After all, the pigs do not turn into alien monsters; they come to resemble those bitter rivals Mr. Pilkington and Mr. Frederick, who represent the Nazis and the Capitalists. All three major "powers" are despicable tyrannies, and the failure of the revolution is not seen in terms of ideology at all, but as a realization of Lord Acton's thesis, "Power tends to corrupt; absolute power corrupts absolutely." The initial spark of a revolution, the original intention of a constitution may have been an ideal of the good life, but the result is always the same—tyranny. Communism is no more or less evil than Fascism or Capitalism—they are all illusions which are inevitably used by the pigs as a means of satisfying their greed and their lust for power. Religion, too, is merely a toy of the oppressors and a device to divert the minds of the sufferers. Moses, the tame raven who is always croaking about the sweet, eternal life in Sugarcandy Mountain, flies after the deposed Farmer Jones, only to return when Napoleon has established his tyranny.

Animal Farm remains powerful satire even as the specific historical events it mocked recede into the past, because the book's major concern is not with these incidents but with the essential horror of the human condition. There have been, are, and always will be pigs in every society, Orwell states, and they will always grab power. Even more cruel is the conclusion that *everyone* in the society, wittingly or unwittingly, contributes to the pigs' tyranny. Boxer, the noblest (though not the wisest) animal on the farm, devotes his unceasing labor to the pigs, who, as has been noted, send him to the knacker when he has outlived his usefulness. There is real pathos as the sound of Boxer's hoofs drumming weakly on the back of the horse slaughterer's van grows fainter and dies away, and the reader senses that in that dying sound is the dying hope of humanity. But Orwell does not allow the mood of oppressive sadness to overwhelm the satire, and Squealer, "lifting his trotter and wiping away a tear," hastens to announce that, after receiving every attention a horse could have, Boxer died in his hospital bed, with the words "Napoleon is always right" on his withered lips. Frederick R. Karl, in *The Contemporary English Novel*, believes that

Animal Farm fails as successful satire "by virtue of its predictability,"[41] but this terrifying predictability of the fate of all revolutions is just the point Orwell is trying to make. The grotesque end of the fable is not meant to shock the reader —indeed, chance and surprise are banished entirely from Orwell's world. The horror of both *Animal Farm* and the later *1984* is precisely the cold, orderly, predictable process by which decency, happiness, and hope are systematically and ruthlessly crushed.

1984 (published in 1949) is Orwell's last novel, and it brings together every strand of his previous work. The black pessimism of this book may be, in part, explained by the fact that Orwell's wife had died suddenly in 1945, that his own health was deteriorating, that he sensed that he was dying, but the mood of suicidal despair which pervades *1984* seems even more to be the result of Orwell's conclusion that he had explored all the so-called solutions to man's misery and found nothing but lies. The whole world, Orwell felt, is steadily moving toward a vast and ruthless tyranny, and there is absolutely nothing that can stop the monstrous progress. *1984*, in spite of its setting in the future, is not primarily a utopian fantasy prophesying what the world will be like in thirty or forty years but a novel about what the world is like now. Hopkinson, discussing what he believes is the failure of *1984*, complains that "Orwell, sick and dispirited, has imagined nothing new . . . His world of 1984 is the war-time world of 1944, but dirtier and more cruel— and with all the endurance and nobility which distinguished mankind in that upheaval, mysteriously drained away. *Everyone* by 1984 is to be a coward, a spy, and a betrayer . . . The horror which distorts life in the future is merely the horror that hangs over life today."[42] It is difficult to respond to a critic like Mr. Hopkinson, for he denies the whole purpose of Orwell's novel, which is to show, by means of the expressionistic device of the utopian novel, "merely the horror

41. Frederick R. Karl, *The Contemporary English Novel* (New York, 1959), p. 163.
42. Hopkinson, p. 35.

that hangs over life today." The contemporary relevance is seen, of course, in the allegory of a world divided into three power blocs—Oceania, Eurasia, and Eastasia—which roughly resemble the present major powers; in the dominant ideology of Oceania, called Ingsoc, which is obviously an abbreviation of English Socialism; in the "history" of the first half of the twentieth century; and in the setting, which Hopkinson points out is so clearly London, 1944. This immediacy, however, is even more apparent in the major themes of the book, which have all been examined, in a more "realistic" context, in Orwell's earlier novels and essays—the disappearance of the heroic, the crushing of the individual, the cynical tampering with history, the contempt for liberty, the inevitable tyranny of the pigs, the physical horror of existence.

1984 is the story of the revolt against society of one man, Winston Smith, but, as in all of Orwell's novels, the environment is far more important than the characters or the plot. The world against which Winston raises his feeble and doomed rebellion is a composite of every hell Orwell ever attempted to portray. It is the dirty, ugly city George Bowling confronted in *Coming Up for Air,* the nightmarish, savage jungle of *Burmese Days,* the squalid slums and doss houses of *Down and Out in Paris and London,* the gloomy subterranean chambers and smoking slag heaps of *The Road to Wigan Pier,* and, above all, the filthy prison-house world of "Such, Such Were the Joys . . ." The spirit of Oceania so closely resembles that of Crossgates school that Anthony West complained that "What Orwell did in *1984* was to send everybody in England to an enormous Crossgates to be as miserable as himself."[43] And indeed, the terrors and pains which afflict Winston Smith are remarkably like those experienced by the young child, overwhelmed by "a sense of desolate loneliness and helplessness, of being locked up not only in a hostile world but in a world of good and evil where the rules were such that it was actually not possible for me to keep them" ("Such, Such Were the Joys . . .," p. 13). Orwell recalls

43. West, quoted in Dooley, p. 293.

that once, when he had broken school rules and bought some chocolates, he noticed a small, sharp-faced man staring very hard at his school cap and was convinced that this man was a spy placed there by Sim, the headmaster: "It did not seem to me strange that the headmaster of a private school should dispose of an army of informers . . . Sim was all-powerful, and it was natural that his agents should be everywhere" (p. 23). In the world of *1984* the tyrant, Big Brother, does employ a vast army of informers, called thought police, who watch every individual at all times for the least signs of criminal deviation, which may consist simply of unorthodox thoughts, let alone buying chocolates without orders.

In spite of the complex mythology of a savior-tyrant and the constant admonitions that "Big Brother Is Watching You," Oceania, like Eurasia and Eastasia, is ruled by a system of oligarchical collectivism, by an all-powerful Party, which has abolished private property and whose members are designated, according to their power and responsibility, Inner Party or Outer Party. The membership of the Party is only 15 per cent of the population; the remaining 85 per cent are the Proles, kept in a state of abject poverty and total ignorance, "prolefed" lies by the Ministry of Truth, terrorized by the Ministry of Love. The economy of Oceania is always on an emergency basis, for there is perpetual war between the three powers, not to win control of the disputed territory between them, but deliberately to perpetuate shortages, to create a horribly low standard of living that will keep the people miserable. As Orwell learned in *Down and Out in Paris and London,* poverty eliminates the possibility of thought, and independent thinking is the greatest danger to the totalitarian states. The goal of the three powers, then, is not victory but everlasting war, and though no contact of any kind is allowed between the states, "as long as they remain in conflict they prop one another up like three sheaves of corn."[44] War, therefore, is essential to the stability of the state, and thus the first basic tenet of Oceania: War Is Peace.

The remaining principles of the totalitarian state are re-

44. Orwell, *1984* (New York, Signet Books, 1949), p. 150.

lated to Orwell's growing concern, in the last years of his life, with the relation between politics and language.[45] If language is abused, if words can have entirely contradictory meanings at the same time, if the language necessary to express political opposition is destroyed, if notions of objective truth and unchanging history are abandoned, then since thought is dependent on language, all unorthodox modes of thought can be made impossible, history can be altered to suit the needs of the moment, the individual can be reduced to an automaton, incapable of thought or disloyalty. Orwell found he could not fully integrate into the plot of *1984* these rather complex reflections on the development of the modern state and its use of language, and so he wisely developed his ideas in two essays, the first inserted in the novel as a heretical book entitled "The Theory and Practice of Oligarchical Collectivism," reputedly by the archenemy of the State, Emmanuel Goldstein, but actually written by the thought police as a trap for Winston. The second essay is placed outside the novel entirely as an Appendix entitled "The Principles of Newspeak."

It is against a vast, ruthless, immensely powerful state that Winston Smith rebels. Like all of Orwell's heroes, Winston is neither glorious, nor brave, nor resourceful, nor even truly rebellious. He is a smallish, frail figure, with a varicose ulcer above his right ankle, false teeth, and, of course, a hyperdeveloped sense of smell. He is frozen by the vile wind, sickened by the heavy odor of boiled cabbage and old rag mats in his hallway and the overpowering smell of sweat of his fat neighbor, nauseated by the regulation lunch—"a pinkish-gray . . . filthy liquid mess that had the appearance of vomit." Winston's revolt is not motivated primarily by love of freedom, belief in the dignity of man, or even sexual passion, but by a lack of discipline, a failure in his education. Like the little boy at Crossgates, he is unable to control his instincts and thus unable to be loyal. The dramatic tension of *1984* is not whether Winston will be able to revolt successfully against the Party, for such revolt is inconceiv-

45. See Orwell, "Politics and the English Language," *Essays*, pp. 162–77.

able. By means of a spying device called a telescreen, the thought police keep all Party members under constant surveillance, and Winston knows that he is doomed from the moment he has his first heretical thought. The tensions of the novel concern how long he can stay alive and whether it is possible for Winston to die without mentally betraying his rebellion.

Winston Smith's active revolt begins with his decision to keep a diary, but it receives its full expression in his love affair with Julia, a co-worker in the Ministry of Truth. Unlike Winston, Julia is not even vaguely interested in politics or ideology. Her heresy is "sexcrime"—she enjoys sexual intercourse. Sex, like the family, represents a threat to the state, because it is essentially private, isolated, uncontrollable. Through a great many maneuvers and subterfuges Winston and Julia manage secretly to arrange meetings and eventually to rent an apartment in a proletarian slum from an antique-shop owner named Charrington. The couple also make contact with O'Brien, a mysterious Inner Party member who tells them he is an agent of Goldstein and enlists them in a Brotherhood dedicated to the overthrow of the party. Winston had thought that the only hope for the overthrow of Big Brother lay in the proles, but O'Brien explains that "from the proletarians nothing is to be feared. Left to themselves, they will continue from generation to generation and from century to century, working, breeding, and dying, not only without any impulse to rebel, but without the power of grasping that the world could be other than it is" (p. 160). If the proles are useless, it is not clear how the Brotherhood will destroy the State, but Winston and Julia promise, nonetheless, that they are fully prepared, if called upon, to murder, to commit acts of sabotage, "to cheat, to forge, to blackmail, to corrupt the minds of children, to distribute habit-forming drugs, to encourage prostitution, to disseminate venereal diseases. . . . to throw sulphuric acid in a child's face" (p. 131). It is clear, of course, that even if there were a Brotherhood based on these principles, it could only replace the tyranny of Big Brother with another as evil. The possibility is never explored, however, because both

Charrington and O'Brien are members of the thought police, the Brotherhood is merely a trap, and Winston and Julia are arrested.

The remainder of *1984* is a record of the total annihilation of Winston Smith, the destruction of his personality, his "reintegration" into society, under the cruel but steady hand of O'Brien. It becomes increasingly apparent in the course of the novel that Big Brother is a surrogate God and that the members of the Inner Party are His priests, and so it is not surprising that O'Brien takes on the role of inquisitor whose duty is to purify Winston by exorcising the demon of heresy. Within this religious context Winston can finally receive the answer to his gnawing question—*Why* does the Party cling to power? Just as in *Keep the Aspidistra Flying*, "money" was substituted for "charity" in the passage from St. Paul, so, in *1984*, "power" is substituted for "God." "God is Power" is the final revelation of *1984*, and thus O'Brien's answer to Winston's "Why?" is simple:

> The Party seeks power entirely for its own sake. We are not interested in the good of others; we are interested solely in power. Not wealth or luxury or long life or happiness; only power, pure power . . . The object of power is power . . . The world that we are preparing [is] a world of victory after victory, triumph after triumph after triumph: an endless pressing, pressing, pressing upon the nerve of power.　　　　　[pp. 200–04]

O'Brien and his colleagues are not men but embodiments of the power principle who, as D. J. Dooley points out, "achieve a vicarious immortality through membership in the Inner Party, since the mind of the Party is collective and immortal."[46]

Winston Smith represents the spirit of man in *1984*, but, as O'Brien relentlessly strips away man's protective clothing, the robes of civilization and culture, the garments of refinement, health, and common sense, the human being is revealed to be nothing more than a vile "bag of filth" (p. 207).

46. Dooley, p. 298.

The description of Winston Smith, dirty, rotting, emaciated, stinking like a goat, confronting himself in a mirror in the Ministry of Love, recalls Swift's description of the revolting Yahoos in *Gulliver's Travels*. Man is repulsive, ugly, stupid, cowardly, filthy, and disgusting. Orwell's triumphant humanism has been destroyed, and all that is left is the final vision of Winston, having betrayed Julia and himself, waiting for the bullet that will end his miserable life, drinking foul gin, crying miserable tears of repentance, loving Big Brother.

One wonders what Orwell would have written after *1984*. Evelyn Waugh found Catholicism and Aldous Huxley discovered his perennial philosophy after *Brave New World* and *Ape and Essence,* but somehow one cannot imagine George Orwell settling back into a warm and cozy orthodoxy of his own. At any rate, Orwell precluded this possibility by moving, against his doctors' orders, to the rough island of Jura in the Inner Hebrides, where his chronic cough developed into tuberculosis. He died in London in January 1950, at the age of 47.

Orwell could never bring himself to say "I accept" in "an epoch of fear, tyranny, and regimentation," an age of:

> concentration camps, rubber truncheons, Hitler, Stalin, bombs, aeroplanes, tinned food, machine guns, putsches, purges, slogans, Bedaux belts, gas masks, submarines, spies, provocateurs, press censorship, secret prisons, aspirins, Hollywood films, and political murders.[47]

Orwell was unwilling, indeed one senses that he was totally unable to resign himself quietly to the grim necessity of such a catalogue of horrors in human society. Desperately, he sought an alternative, an instrument of change, a means of relief, but his keen perception of hypocrisy and fraud, his unfailing hatred of injustice and tyranny, his morbidly sensitive nose for rottenness and the vile smells of humanity sys-

47. Orwell, "Inside the Whale," *Essays*, p. 223.

tematically destroyed every system, every ideology, every code that presented itself as a palliative for man's suffering. Orwell's work is the unspeakably sad record of a completely uprooted individual, a man plagued by fundamental moral confusion, driven by a passion for clarity and certainty in a hopelessly confused society, tormented by the burning need for personal commitment in a world where worth-while causes had ceased to exist.

3 ALDOUS HUXLEY

Novel of ideas. *The character of each personage must be implied as far as possible, in the ideas of which he is the mouthpiece. In so far as theories are rationalizations of sentiments, instincts, dispositions of soul, this is feasible. The chief defect of the novel of ideas is that you must write about people who have ideas to express—which excludes all but about .01 per cent of the human race. Hence the real, the congenital novelists don't write such books. But then, I never pretended to be a congenital novelist. . . . The great defect of the novel of ideas is that it is a made-up affair. Necessarily; for people who can reel off neatly formulated notions aren't quite real; they're slightly monstrous. Living with monsters becomes rather tiresome in the long run.*[1]

These reflections by Aldous Huxley on his own art, thinly disguised in *Point Counter Point* as an entry in Philip Quarles' notebook, are eloquent testimony that, as Desmond MacCarthy suggests, "there is little that the critic can tell Mr. Aldous Huxley about his work that he does not already know himself."[2] But the presence of such self-criticism does not exorcise the faults expressed.

Huxley's lucid remarks account for a great deal of the uneasiness one feels in reading his novels. They are, indeed, largely "made-up affairs," with paper-thin characters who live in a world which often seems to be little more than a colossal debating society or an everlasting tea party. Huxley is not terribly concerned with the great social and political issues of his time. Unlike Orwell, he is not outraged by the plight of the common man, not haunted by the specters of oppression and tyranny, not under the compulsion to be a pamphleteer or a revolutionary. Huxley is concerned, rather, with the Bright Young People and their eccentric parents who fascinate Evelyn Waugh; he writes of the sophisticates and intellectuals who flit irresponsibly through the maze of London society. Huxley does not feel comfortable in doss

1. Aldous Huxley, *Point Counter Point* (New York, 1928), p. 307.
2. Desmond MacCarthy, *Criticism* (London, 1932), p. 244.

houses and slums, does not write well about torture and rebellion, and physical pain, but prefers expensive restaurants and country estates, witty conversation, and delicate love affairs. In his novels there are few of the filthy details, little of the physical disgust, and nothing of the furious indignation that characterize Orwell's work, but only the clash of ideas and attitudes, the tensions of conflicting philosophies. Yet, in spite of the artificiality and the unreality of Huxley's novels, they contain much that is brilliant and powerful, for beneath the slick surface of wit and erudition there is a cold and bitter examination of society and its sickness. To appreciate Huxley, one must go beyond the novel of ideas; one must see that Huxley's characters are not monstrous because they can reel off neatly formulated notions, but spout their precious ideas *because* they are monsters. The tendency of Huxlean characters to talk endlessly and accomplish nothing is not a lapse in the author's style but a symptom of the disease which afflicts society. With Huxley, as with Waugh and Orwell, technique and meaning merge in the totality of the novel.

A major problem in Huxley's novels is tone. George Orwell always made his personal position, his likes and dislikes, perfectly obvious; but Huxley is more subtle and detached, contriving to hide his own judgment behind the mass of contradictory opinions and emotions expressed in his books. The tone of satiric novels like *Crome Yellow* (1922), *Antic Hay* (1923), and *Brave New World* (1932) lies somewhere between anger and amusement, disgust and fascination, but, like an unstable chemical element, it can never be precisely fixed or characterized. Huxley's ability to balance conflicting ideological claims, to fathom and to express coherently contradictory opinions, to manipulate subtly the tone of his novels is impressive, but these same qualities are manifestations of a fundamental flaw in his writing—the inability to adopt a clear position. The problem is more complex than simply finding an appealing doctrine or attitude—Huxley's brilliant mind is able to assimilate all doctrines, all attitudes. His comprehensive intelligence enables him to see the world with a multiplicity of eyes, but, like his character Philip

Quarles in *Point Counter Point,* he cannot tell which vision
is truly his own:

> Pascal had made him a Catholic—but only so long as
> the volume of *Pensees* was open before him. There were
> moments when, in the company of Carlyle or Whitman
> or bouncing Browning, he had believed in strenuousness
> for strenuousness' sake. And then there was Mark
> Rampion. After a few hours in Mark Rampion's com-
> pany he really believed in noble savagery . . . But always,
> whatever he might do, he knew quite well in the secret
> depths of his being that he wasn't a Catholic, or a strenu-
> ous liver, or a mystic, or a noble savage.   [pp. 204–05]

When Huxley's novels fail, it is because of the author's
amoeboid mind. A successful satirist must have a limited
point of view, to which he is devoted and by which he assesses
all human behavior. Huxley is profoundly aware of the sickness of society, but he cannot settle his mind on a standard
of judgment. The "multiplicity of eyes" the author strives
for is ultimately destructive to many of his novels, because
Huxley is temperamentally unable to choose between them.
In spite of this confusion, however, there are certain satirical
themes which run throughout his work and unify his novels.
In this chapter I shall attempt to isolate and trace these
themes in a few of the early satires.

Huxley's first novel, *Crome Yellow,* is an irreverent chronicle of that venerable English institution, the week-end party.
The book's outline is exceedingly simple. Old and eccentric
Mrs. Henry Wimbush, who dabbles in horse-racing and as-
trology, invites a group of arty people for a week end at
Crome Manor, a fine country estate. In the course of the novel
the guests are overheard talking about love, sex, art, psychol-
ogy, themselves, and their friends, and, in the process, reveal
the absurd preoccupations and posturings of their set. The
main character, Denis Stone, is a young, self-conscious novelist who makes a number of amusing and unsuccessful attempts to win the love of Anne, a rather shallow but charming hedonist, and finally sends a telegram to himself calling

him back to London. There is no dramatic tension, no climax, no dénouement, no sense of being poised on the brink of an abyss or of being a spectator of a modern Inferno. Rather, *Crome Yellow* is the record of an elaborate social game, a dance, contrived and unreal as all such entertainments must be, but with its own grace and fascination. In leaving London for the serenity of Crome, the characters abandon a brutal, harsh, mechanical reality for a delicate world of indolence and good conversation, of infinite leisure and irresponsibility. Occasionally there are reminders of the unpleasantness of the outside world; but within the walls of the estate such horrors can be rationalized away:

> "At this very moment," Mr. Scogan went on, "the most frightful horrors are taking place in every corner of the world. People are being crushed, slashed, disembowelled, mangled; their dead bodies rot and their eyes decay with the rest. Screams of pain and fear go pulsing through the air at the rate of eleven hundred feet per second. After travelling for three seconds they are perfectly inaudible. These are distressing facts; but do we enjoy life any the less because of them? Most certainly we do not . . . A really sympathetic race would not so much as know the meaning of happiness. But luckily, as I've already said, we aren't a sympathetic race."[3]

The awareness of evil and suffering does not affect the sheltered inhabitants of Crome Manor. It merely establishes an ironic contrast to their little society, much as, in Pope's *The Rape of the Lock*, the awareness of a world in which "hungry Judges soon the sentence sign, / and wretches hang that jurymen may dine" serves as a brief but effective reminder of the artificiality of the heroine's world.

A publicity release that describes *Crome Yellow* as "a bold exploration into love and sex . . . which struck the reading public like a bolt of lightning . . . and shocked and enlightened a generation" demonstrates an incredible insensitivity

---

3. Huxley, *Crome Yellow* (New York, Bantam Books, 1959), p. 77.

to or conscious distortion of the tone and intent of the novel. Mary Bracegirdle's adolescent and quite humorous reflections on free love are the only possible suggestions of the "bold exploration" of sex which the publisher heralds. *Crome Yellow* is hardly a shocking novel. Rather, it is an attempt to portray a group of people who can no longer cope with the harsh necessities of nature and who are trying to remove themselves from all shocks and all unpleasantness into a sunlit world of intellectual refinement.

The merit of *Crome Yellow* and of much of Huxley's writing resides chiefly in the wonderfully humorous caricatures of the participants in the various societal dances. Huxley has a superb facility for finding the concise phrase which sums up the entire character—"Barbeque Smith was a name in the Sunday papers. He wrote about the Conduct of Life. He might even be the author of *What a Young Girl Ought to Know*" (p. 7), or "Mary Bracegirdle's face shone pink and childish . . . Her short hair, clipped like a page's, hung in a bell of elastic gold about her cheeks" (p. 10), or "In appearance Mr. Scogan was like one of those extinct bird-lizards of the tertiary" (p. 10). *Crome Yellow* is filled with a great many of these little portraits, but there is only one character developed in depth in the novel, Denis. With a surprising measure of sympathy and even affection, Huxley portrays this callow young man who "was twenty-three, and oh! so agonizingly conscious of the fact" (p. 1) and who felt weighted down with "great thick books about the universe and the mind and ethics. . . . Twenty tons of ratiocination" (p. 17). Poor, unhappy Denis wishes so much to be a romantic hero, but he succeeds only in making a fool of himself. When Anne twists her ankle, Denis insists upon carrying her back to the house: "stooping he picked her up under the knees and lifted her from the ground. Good heavens, what a weight! He took five staggering steps up the slope, then almost lost his equilibrium, and had to deposit his burden suddenly, with something of a bump" (p. 84).

Crome Yellow, despite its uncharacteristic leniency and even sentimentality, has within it the seeds of much of Huxley's later work, both in form and content. The novel has no real plot, a peculiarity that is both a serious defect and an important characteristic of all Huxley's satires. Like Evelyn Waugh in *Vile Bodies,* Huxley is writing about people who have lost the ability to act meaningfully, to create, to generate; people who can do nothing but expound clever theories or witty commentaries which the reader senses have all been prepared months before and rehearsed a hundred times. Not only have all the characters retreated into the artificial world of Crome Manor, but they have walled themselves within their own intellects and have cut themselves off from their fellow humans. "We are all parallel straight lines," reflects Denis, and, indeed, in spite of the immense quantity of talk, there is no real communication between the characters.

Huxley also displays in his first novel something of the verbal brilliance, precocity, and immense erudition of his encyclopedic mind, which later become almost overwhelming in *Point Counter Point*. Caesar Borgia, St. Francis, and Dr. Johnson all find their way into the conversation at Crome Manor, along with such varied and obscure literary figures as Squire, Binyon, Shanks, Childe, Blunden, Earp, Abercrombie, Drinkwater, and Rabindranath Tagore. The very unlikeliness of this group gives the reader the impression that Huxley is mocking his own vast, clearinghouse mind, at the same time that he is employing it to create the arty, intellectual atmosphere at Crome.

Striking evidence of the manner in which certain themes slowly matured in Huxley's mind are the prophetic reflections of old Mr. Scogan who describes the rational "paradise" of the future:

> An impersonal generation will take the place of Nature's hideous system. In vast state incubators, rows upon rows of gravid bottles will supply the world with the population it requires. The family system will disappear: society, sapped at its very base, will have to find new foundations; and eros, beautifully and irresponsibly free, will flit like a gay butterfly from flower to flower through a sunlit world. [p. 22]

The dangers of man's obsession with progress, however, are only glimpsed in *Crome Yellow*. Ten years later this fleeting vision had matured into the terrifying *Brave New World*.

The most interesting and most often misinterpreted feature in *Crome Yellow* is the rather strange "History of Crome," appearing intermittently in anecdotes throughout the novel. In short installments read by old Mr. Wimbush from his enormous hobbyhorse, "The History of Crome Manor," the lives of the various inhabitants of the house from the seventeenth century to the twentieth are briefly sketched. At first glance, these beautifully written accounts seem arbitrarily inserted into the novel without real relevance to its meaning; indeed, most critics deplore the "History" as an unnecessary interruption. Pelham Edgar writes that "In *Crome Yellow* the progress of the story is . . . delayed while the author inserts . . . excellent short stories designed as extracts from the 'History.' They are gems in the fantastic style, but they have nothing to do with *Crome Yellow*."[4] And, in the opinion of Sisirkumar Ghose, the "History" is "delicately spiced, runny, but altogether an interior piece. It has really no connection with the rest of the novel."[5] Finally, Jocelyn Brooke chooses to ignore entirely the series of tales.[6]

The whole point of *Crome Yellow* has been missed if the excerpts from the "History" are not appreciated. The group assembled at Crome Manor in 1922 are the direct spiritual descendants of generations of past inhabitants. From the laying of the first massive block of stone in the seventeenth century, Crome was an insolent revolt against nature. The architect and builder, Sir Ferdinando Lapith, was obsessed with the brutishness of the bodily functions, so unbefitting the noblest creatures of the universe:

> To counteract these degrading effects he advised that
> the privy should be in every house the room nearest to
> heaven, that it should be well provided with windows

4. Pelham Edgar, *The Art of the Novel* (New York, 1933), p. 283.
5. Sisirkumar Ghose, *Aldous Huxley* (New York, 1962), p. 158.
6. Jocelyn Brooke, *Aldous Huxley* (London, 1954).

commanding an extensive and noble prospect, and that the walls of the chamber should be lined with bookshelves containing all the ripest products of human wisdom . . . which testify to the nobility of the human soul. [p. 48]

With this brilliant innovation, man, even while performing his most natural and humbling duties, can look from a lordly height down at inferior nature. Truly, as Mr. Scogan observes, Crome Manor "makes no compromise with nature, but affronts it and rebels against it."

From the ingenious arrogance of the seventeenth century, Huxley moves to the next century and the strange story of Hercules Lapith. Hercules, a dwarf, contrives to shield himself from the scorn of the vulgar and insensitive giants around him by marrying a beautiful Italian princess of similar proportions and retreating to Crome Manor, where the couple create a delicate world in miniature—dwarfed servants, specially constructed furniture, a string of Shetland ponies for rabbit hunts, etc. The couple live blissfully isolated from the rest of mankind for a number of years and are thrilled when graced with the birth of a son whom, in joyous expectation, they plan to introduce to the beauties of their unnatural but superior world. To their dismay, their son, Ferdinando, turns out to be of the "normal gigantic dimensions," and, while they forestall the inevitable unhappy conclusion by sending him on a grand tour, it is evident that their tiny, fragile world has been shattered. When, one evening soon after Ferdinando has returned home, Hercules spies his son and his school chums cruelly baiting the little family butler, Hercules realizes that "this was the end; there was no place for him now in the world, no place for him and Ferdinando together" (p. 67). Stealing upstairs, he reminisces sentimentally with his wife and then gives her a lethal sleeping draught. Quietly he retires to his bath, slits his wrists, and "dies like a noble Roman."

The story of Hercules, delicately blending irony and pathos, is among the finest writing Huxley ever did. E. B. Burgum in *The Novel and the World's Dilemma,* claims that it is "only too clear that the dwarf represents his (Huxley's) essential self," and that this identification enabled the author to write "with a depth of emotion he was never afterwards to achieve and a directness he has never cared to repeat."[7] There is, indeed, much feeling in the story of Hercules, but it is a mistake, I think, to get carried away with the pathos of the dwarf's fate and to conceive of the little tale as tragic or autobiographical. This vignette, like the rest of the "History of Crome," is an ironic comment on man's absurd pretensions. Tiny Hercules, building a miniature world around himself and composing heroic couplets which celebrate his smallness, is Huxley's image of the whole eighteenth century, glorying in its artificiality, pleased with its pygmy stature.

The final vignette from Mr. Wimbush's "History" takes place, as we should expect, in the nineteenth century and concerns the three lovely daughters of Ferdinando. The girls are self-proclaimed romantics and are so immersed in reflections on Transcendence and the Soul that they chose to ignore their bodily existence entirely. Their concern for pure spirituality is so great, in fact, that they refuse to eat more than a few insubstantial morsels, "waving away whatever was offered them with an expression of delicate disgust":

> "Pray, don't talk to me of eating," said Emmeline, drooping like a sensitive plant. "We find it so coarse, so unspiritual, my sisters and I. One can't think of one's soul while one is eating."[8]   [p. 94]

But the girls' imposing spirituality is exposed as mere sham, for, in secret, they gorge themselves with a gusto and an "earthy" enthusiasm they would be ashamed to admit to in society.

The three anecdotes from the "History of Crome Manor" are interesting in their own right (the tale of Hercules was published in a separate collection of short stories), but placed

7. Edwin Berry Burgum, *The Novel and the World's Dilemma* (New York, 1947), pp. 144-45.
8. The image of the sensitive plant is a fine Huxlean touch, alluding ironically to Shelley's eminently romantic poem "The Sensitive Plant."

together in *Crome Yellow,* they take on a new significance. Behind a front of nostalgia and sheer fun, Huxley is presenting an allegory of man's relationship with nature through the centuries. From the insolence of the builder of Crome in the seventeenth century, through the delicate artificiality of the eighteenth, through the spurious romanticism of the nineteenth, and into the hyperintellectualism of the twentieth, man has been living on bad terms with nature and with himself. The world makes man feel uncomfortable, degraded, lonely, afraid; and so he builds an artificial world, not just with bricks and mortar, but with ideas. Mr. Scogan frankly admits to the falseness of these structures, but prefers the safe, man-made shelters to the jungle of reality:

> Nature, or anything that reminds me of nature, disturbs me; it is too large, too complicated, above all too utterly pointless and incomprehensible. I am at home with the works of man: if I choose to set my mind to it, I can understand anything that any man has made or thought. That is why I always travel by Tube, never by bus if I can possibly help it. For, travelling by bus, one can't avoid seeing, even in London, a few stray works of God —the sky, for example, an occasional tree, the flowers in the window-boxes. But travel by Tube and you see nothing but the works of man—iron riveted into geometrical forms, straight lines of concrete, patterned expanse of tiles. All is human and the product of friendly and comprehensible minds. [p. 118]

This remarkable passage is absolutely central to all of Huxley's work, for Scogan eloquently articulates the problem faced by each Huxlean hero and, indeed, by the author himself. Man is thrown into a vast and indifferent universe, which he doesn't comprehend but in which he must somehow survive. Scogan, like the past and present inhabitants of Crome, is incapable of integrating his life with this natural world. Brilliant and perceptive, he is well aware of the artificiality of his society and of the "Rational State" he prophesies (which very much resembles the Brave New World), but he arrogantly turns his back on nature and cynically exalts the falsehood which is Crome.[9] Huxley rejects the whole notion of progress, for Crome is no different in 1920 than in the seventeenth century—man has had no success in learning to live in and with nature. If anything, the modern generation is worse than the previous ones, for arrogant pride and heroism have given way to self-indulgence and the "twenty tons of ratiocination."

We are now in a position to understand why Huxley's characters talk so much—in spinning out their elaborate theories, they are spinning out the protective cocoons which shelter them from the harshness of nature. As Mr. Scogan explains:

> All philosophies and all religions—what are they but spiritual tubes bored through the universe! Through these narrow tunnels, where all is recognisably human, one travels comfortable and secure, contriving to forget that all round and below and above them stretches the blind mass of earth, endless and unexplored. [p. 118]

Huxley insists upon a complete dichotomy of intellect and nature (truth, spirit, reality). The world of ideas is snug but false, neat but artificial, simple and well made but detrimental to man's good. "One entered the world, Denis pursued, having ready-made ideas about everything. One had a philosophy and tried to make life fit into it. One should have lived first and then made one's philosophy to fit life. . . . Life, facts, things were horribly complicated; ideas, even the most difficult of them, deceptively simple. In the world of ideas everything was clear; in life all was obscure, embroiled. Was it surprising that one was miserable, horribly unhappy?" (p. 17). Thought tears man away from the true reality of his physical existence. Theories of soul, human nobility, God are merely escape mechanisms from the brutal but real

9. While Huxley seems to reject Scogan's ideas and, with them, rejects intellectualism, the reader is left with an uncomfortable sense that Huxley is of Scogan's party without knowing it. One's suspicions are confirmed by Huxley's discovery, many years later, of his own cozy, metaphysical shelter—the Perennial Philosophy.

world. Unfortunately, the ability to live in good faith is hard to come by. The prejudices of a Christian education which denies the importance of this world are firmly implanted and all but impossible to destroy.

The vision of nature that underlies Huxley's satire is neither the nature of brute, animal existence nor the scientist's cold, unfeeling universe, but a sort of romantic conception of nature as the embodiment of a Universal Mind. In spite of his criticism of Wordsworth for making the world seem too cozy and benevolent, Huxley perceives "something far more deeply interfused" in the natural scene—something not humanized or even friendly to man, but a realm that transcends the human experience and fuses individual identity into a vast organic whole. In a late essay entitled "The Desert," Huxley attempts to characterize this other realm:

> Nature is blessedly non-human; and insofar as we belong to the natural order, we too are blessedly non-human. The otherness of caterpillars, as of our own bodies, is an otherness underlain by a principal identity. The non-humanity of wild flower, as of the deepest levels of our own minds, exists within a system which includes and transcends the human. In the given realm of the inner and outer non-self, we are all one. In the home-made realm of symbols we are separate and mutually hostile partisans. Thanks to words, we have been able to rise above the brutes; and thanks to words, we have often sunk to the level of the demons.[10]

Much has happened to Huxley's thought by the time he writes this passage in *Tomorrow and Tomorrow and Tomorrow,* and he has adopted the language of mysticism, but, even in 1922 he conceived of nature as a realm of nonverbal communication, a realm where the artificiality and isolation and futility of man's existence have disappeared. Unfortunately, the author himself does not know how to attain such happiness, and the natural life remains a distant ideal.

10. Huxley, "The Desert," *Collected Essays* (New York, 1960, Bantam Classic), pp. 25–26.

From the quiet and sheltered world of Crome Manor with its air of a living antique, Huxley suddenly turns to the frenzied horrors of London in the postwar Jazz Age. In a terrifying and grossly stupid Inferno, mankind dances its meaningless tarantella. Written with a marvelous intensity and vigor which does not once wane, *Antic Hay,* published a scant year after *Crome Yellow,* is a brutal shock, a hard slap at accepted values. If literature is, in Kafka's words, "a scream," *Antic Hay* is a piercing and agonized one. Gone are the easy leniency, the whimsicality, the amused sympathy of *Crome Yellow,* and in their place is an intense bitterness and despair. Perhaps I am overemphasizing the blackness of *Antic Hay;* critics are quick to point out the comicality of the novel, and Philip Henderson even suggests that it is "all rather good fun."[11] But the laughter is alternately delirious, hysterical, sinister, cynical, diabolical, false—anything but happy. As one of the characters remarks, "Every one's a walking farce and a walking tragedy at the same time. The man who slips on a banana-skin and fractures his skull describes against the sky, as he falls, the most richly comical arabesque."[12]

The fundamental theme of *Antic Hay* is the disintegration of natural values and the subsequent meaninglessness of existence. Huxley does not attempt to explain this sorry world or to offer any solutions; he merely pictures it in all its grotesque misery. The characters run desperately from one scene of debauchery to another in a frantic search for divertissement, for release from the terrible ennui of a sterile civilization. In a society where "men like satyrs grazing on the lawns / Shall with their goat-feet dance the antic hay,"[13] there has been a total breakdown of communication. As always, people talk endlessly—about love, sex, education, politics, physiology, art—but there is absolutely no exchange of ideas. Significantly, *Antic Hay* lacks even the tenuous unifying factor of the week-end tea party at Crome Manor.

11. Philip Henderson, *The Novel Today* (London, 1936), p. 119.
12. Huxley, *Antic Hay* (New York, 1923), p. 275.
13. Inscription by Marlowe, used by Huxley in *Antic Hay.*

People merely come together for a few hours at a restaurant, a bar, or a night club, and then separate as abruptly as they met. There are no identifying bonds between the characters.

The plot outline of *Antic Hay* is significant only in its insignificance. In the world Huxley presents there are no plots, no unified adventures, no meaningful actions, no climax, no dénouement. What exists is only a casual narrative, a gruesome picaresque with separate scenes connected only by the consistent tone of bitterness and disillusionment and by the central characters. As *Antic Hay* opens, Theodore Gumbril Junior, B.A. Oxon, a young man of modest means and a desire to avoid responsibility, gives up his ushership at a prep school and proceeds to live a confused and degenerate life with his friends, shuttling from restaurant to cabaret to bedroom. Between witty conversation and various experiments in passion, he manages to invent and sell a patent for pneumatic underclothes which place a bladder of air between a man's hindquarters and the world—another sly, ironic instance of man's separation from nature. At the close of the book, Gumbril, to relieve his boredom, is off to the Continent to promote his patent.

The characters, almost without exception, are obsessed with the complete inconsequence and hopelessness of their lives. Their devotion to sophistication and modernity has rendered ideals totally impossible. " 'But really,' Gumbril insisted, 'you can't say "dream." . . . Not in this year of grace, nineteen twenty-two. . . . After you've accepted the war, swallowed the Russian Famine. . . . Now the word merely connotes Freud' " (p. 54). Science and skepticism have destroyed all meaning for these disillusioned sophisticates. They have lost all sense of the continuity of history; in fact, they have lost all sense of history itself. The characters of *Antic Hay* are totally uprooted; their lives have been completely dissociated from the values of the past, and all that remains is an everlasting futility. As Coleman, the diabolist, relates, "I used to hang about the biological laboratories at school, eviscerating frogs—crucified with pins, they were, belly upwards, like little green Christs—I remember once, when I was sitting there, quietly poring over the entrails, in came the laboratory boy and said to the stinks usher: 'Please, sir, may I have the key of the Absolute?' . . . But it was only the absolute alcohol the urchin wanted—to pickle some loathsome foetus in, I suppose" (p. 62). The inhabitants of Huxley's world desperately need ideals, but there is nothing left for them. All that they see is "Nil, omnipresent nil, world soul, spiritual informer of all matter. . . . Nothing at all" (p. 216).

Antic Hay (1923) strongly resembles T. S. Eliot's *The Waste Land*, published a year earlier. Huxley's universe is the "heap of broken images," London is the "Unreal city, / Under the brown fog of a winter dawn," with crowds flowing everywhere and nowhere, and the song of the Negro minstrels in the unlicensed cabaret—"What's he to Hecuba? Nothing at all"—is surely "that Shakespeherian Rag." The smell of death is everywhere, and the specter of nothingness informs all.

The characters' reactions to the vacuum in which they find themselves are all different but uniformly unsatisfying. Mercaptan,[14] whose "alas! too snoutlike nose" is inconsistent with his philosophy of life, glories in being "civilized," in "my little rococo boudoir, and the conversations across polished mahogany, and the delicate, lascivious, witty little flirtations on ample sofas inhabited by the soul of Crebillon Fils" (p. 55). The reaction of the artist, Casimir Lypiatt, to Mercaptan's way of life may be taken as Huxley's:

> You disgust me—you and your odious little sham eighteenth-century civilization; your piddling little poetry; your art for art's sake . . . your nauseating little copulations without love or passion; your hoggish materialism; your bestial indifference to all that's unhappy and your yelping hatred of all that's great.
>
> [p. 56]

Unfortunately, Lypiatt's definition of great is Casimir Lypiatt. Behind his Titanic front of the "solitary giant" who

14. "Mercaptan," incidentally, is the chemical name for an evil-smelling sulfur compound.

has set himself "to restore painting and poetry to their rightful position among the great moral forces," hides a pitiful fool who has never grown out of his adolescent egotism and inferiority complex. As one of the characters remarks, Lypiatt's life, like his art, has no life but much posturing. This theme of masks is an important one in *Antic Hay*—practically every character in the novel tries to hide from others and from himself the anguish and despair in his soul.

Coleman, the satanist, however, devotes himself to a blasphemous and masochistic debauchery which he knows is meaningless, but which he cultivates just for that reason. " 'The real charm about debauchery,' said Coleman philosophically, 'is its total pointlessness, futility, and above all its incredible tediousness.' " By cultivating the most unpleasant habits and beliefs, this modern Baudelaire is able to attain the delicious pleasure of punishing himself and being aware of it. He even cultivates a belief in God, so that he can truly know the anguish of sin and can wallow in "wounds big enough to let a coach-and-six drive into their purulent recesses" (p. 286). But Coleman's dishonesty and bad faith is the greatest of all the characters, for, not finding the easy meaning he hoped for in life, he has given up the search and has embarked on a senseless spiting of the world and of himself.

Shearwater, the physiologist, immerses himself into science. The more confusing his world becomes, the more strange variables appear which he did not account for, the deeper he escapes into a grotesque and absurd irreality. The total meaninglessness of his twisted science can be seen in the animals "devoted to the service of physiology: . . . the albino guinea pigs peered through the meshes of their hutch and their red eyes were like the rear lights of bicycles. . . . The cock into which Shearwater had engrafted an ovary came out, not knowing whether to crow or cluck . . . The beetles who had had their heads cut off and replaced by the heads of other beetles, darted uncertainly about, some obeying their heads, some their genital organs" (pp. 326–27). In the midst of this bizarre menagerie sits Shearwater whose ceaseless activity in the experimental chamber called a "hot-box" is the crucial metaphor for the entire world of *Antic Hay:*

> Shearwater sat on his stationary bicycle, pedalling unceasingly like a man in a nightmare. The pedals were geared to a little wheel under the saddle and the rim of the wheel rubbed, as it revolved against a brake, carefully adjusted to make the work of the pedaller hard, but not impossibly hard. From a pipe which came up through the floor issued a little jet of water which played on the brake and kept it cool. But no jet of water played on Shearwater. It was his business to get hot. He did get hot. . . . Great drops of sweat came oozing out from under his hair, ran down over his forehead, hung beaded on his eyebrows, ran into his eyes, down his nose, along his cheeks, fell like raindrops. His thick bull-neck was wet; his whole naked body, his arms and legs streamed and shone. The automatically controlled heating apparatus in the basement kept the temperature in the box high and steady . . . Another time . . . They'd make the box airtight and see the effect of a little carbon dioxide poisoning on top of excessive sweating.
>
> [pp. 321–22]

Shearwater's ceaseless pedaling is symbolic of the futile struggles of all the characters, shut up in their own hot-boxes, seated on their own bicycles, escaping each from his own problems, pedaling and sweating and never getting anywhere. One must note that the hot-boxes are all man-made. In fact, they are expressly constructed to shut man off from the complexities of his real life. Shearwater's laboratory is a distorted and scientific Crome Manor.

Gumbril, the hero of *Antic Hay,* is the only major character who has not fully capitulated to the hot-boxes. To be sure, he cultivates his own mask (a very real one—the false beard he puts on to act the complete man), but at least, like Denis Stone, he is aware of how unsatisfactory his life is. Unfortunately, he is too paralyzed by disillusionment to change his ways, to extricate himself from the web of Nil.

There are, however, a few small glimpses of hope. Gumbril has a rather pathetic but beautiful affair (platonic) with Emily:

> Very gently, he began caressing her shoulder, her long slender arm, drawing his finger-tips lightly and slowly over her smooth skin; slowly from her neck, over her shoulder, lingeringly round the elbow to her hand. Again, again: he was learning her arm. The form of it was part of the knowledge, now, of his finger-tips; his fingers knew it as they knew a piece of music, as they knew Mozart's Twelfth Sonata, for example. And the themes that crowd so quickly one after another at the beginning of the first movement played themselves aerially, glitteringly in his mind; they became part of the enchantment. [p. 198]

This passage is significant for both technique and meaning. It presages Huxley's theory of the "musicalization of fiction," the description of one experience in terms of another, which is the central figure in *Point Counter Point*. Furthermore, it suggests the positive vision of which *Antic Hay* is the satiric antithesis. What Emily and Gumbril achieve for a brief moment and then lose is a quiet, natural communication without words, grandiose gestures, scientific detachment. In this beautiful telepathy they resemble the starlings that Gumbril Senior describes lovingly: "Not having the wit to invent a language or an expressive pantomime, they contrive to communicate such simple thoughts as they have directly and instantaneously. . . . Without a leader, without a word of command, they do everything together, in complete unison. Sitting here in the evenings, I sometimes fancy I can feel their thoughts striking against my own" (p. 317). But most men are afraid of this awesome silent communion—it makes them feel too alone, too naked. And so, they order the machines to grind, the jazz band to play, the minstrels to howl, and the wild, delirious antic hay begins again.

Gumbril is talked into abandoning Emily by Mrs. Viveash, the sophisticated femme fatale, and he once again "glories in the name of earwig," in a life without meaning, an insect existence. The last scene of the book is an endless, futile circular taxi ride through the filthy streets of London:

> "Tomorrow," said Gumbril at last, meditatively. "To-morrow," Mrs. Viveash interrupted him, "will be as awful as today." She breathed it like a truth from beyond the grave, prematurely revealed, expiringly from her deathbed within.   [p. 327]

Although all of his fiction has strong ironic elements, Aldous Huxley did not write satire exclusively, and his next truly satirical novel is not, I believe, *Those Barren Leaves* (1925) or the long, semi-autobiographical *Point Counter Point* (1928), but *Brave New World* (1932), published almost ten years after *Antic Hay*. Huxley has stated that a utopian novel by H. G. Wells was the motivation for *Brave New World;* but it is obvious that the dangers of scientific materialism, blind faith in progress, and hedonism had long been troubling him, and his concern finally found full expression in this fine novel. In *Brave New World* Huxley has managed to sustain a structural simplicity and dynamism he sorely lacked in earlier works. He has also divested himself of the aura of the Jazz Age that has rather dated the novels of the 1920s, while retaining all of his standard devices of irony and satire—the contrapuntal themes, the dizzy piling up of arguments and incidents, the witty caricatures. More important, working in a definite framework—the utopian novel —he is able to integrate fully his great talent for fantasy which he exhibited in "The History of Crome Manor" and his brilliant and bitter social criticism.

Point Counter Point is prefaced with lines by Greville which express the basic problem of all of Huxley's characters:

> O, wearisome conditions of humanity!
> Born under one law, to another bound,
> Vainly begot and yet forbidden vanity:
> Created sick, commanded to be sound.
> What meaneth Nature by these diverse laws—
> Passion and reason, self-division's cause?

In *Brave New World* this self-division is allegorized and forced to its ultimate conclusions. The realms of reason and passion are totally apart in Huxley's utopia, passion having been vanquished and exiled to a few remote, forbidding corners of the world. It is important to note that passion, for Huxley, is not necessarily or even probably gratification and pleasure, physical or otherwise. Rather, it is a sort of primal, *natural* emotion, which man experiences when he achieves profound union with nature. It is also important to see that *Brave New World,* like Orwell's *1984,* is primarily concerned not with what will happen in the future but what is happening to mankind now. A futuristic detail like the hatching of babies from bottles, for example, is less an interesting scientific speculation than an ironic comment on the dissociation of sexuality and childbirth and on the ultimate artificiality of the inhabitants of our brave new world.

The principles of reason, as seen by Huxley, are embodied in the Brave New World that is the realization of Mr. Scogan's "Rational State." The basic goal of this state is the happiness of all, even if this happiness is purchased at the cost of imagination, discovery, free will, poetry, and pure science. The Trinity of the world state is "Community, Identity, Stability," and to achieve these ends, life is totally planned, *ab ovo.* Citizens of this "last word in organized good times and of secular revolutions"[15] are hatched from bottles and predetermined as members of a strictly defined caste— alpha, beta, gamma, delta, or epsilon. Women undergo an "Operation . . . voluntarily for the good of Society, not to mention the fact that it carries a bonus amounting to six months' salary," and the remarkable "Bokanovsky's Process" successfully produces "scores of standard men and women from the same ovary and with gametes of the same male." By means of mass suggestion during sleep and other devious psychological techniques, the children are completely reconciled to their own caste and are given a strong aversion for beauty, art, and solitude. In their place are endless rounds of promiscuity and meaningless games, as well as "liquid air,

15. Ghose, *Aldous Huxley,* p. 50.

television, vibro-vacuum massage, radio, boiling caffeine solution, hot contraceptives, and eight different kinds of scent . . . in every bedroom."[16] The creatures of this world are doomed to be happy. No other kind of life is possible or imaginable. And if any vexations arise—like the mention of the obscene word "mother" or the arousal of a passion— there are always the pregnancy substitutes, the V.P.S. ("Violent Passion Surrogate—the complete physiological equivalent of fear and rage. All the tonic effects of murdering Desdemona and being murdered by Othello without any of the inconveniences"), and of course, that most delightful of all wonder drugs, soma ("All the advantages of Christianity and alcohol; none of their defects."). Such is the state of the world in the year 623 After-Ford ("Our Ford—or Our Freud, as, for some inscrutable reason, he chose to call himself whenever he spoke of psychological matters" is the deity of the Rational State). Man, in using his reason to create the ultimate life of pleasure, has ceased to be man.

Into this realm of unceasing and sterile happiness comes the Savage, the natural-born son of Linda, an ex-beta-minus who was abandoned on an Indian Reservation by the man who was "having" her for the week end, and discovered by Bernard Marx, one of the rare deviants from the Fordian norm (rumored cause—"alcohol in his blood surrogate"). The Savage has many unheard-of qualities and strange habits —he quotes Shakespeare, actually *loves* his mother, is a romantic, and believes in God. Living on the reservation, he is also disease-ridden, unhappy, filthy, and masochistic. Brought to London by Bernard, the Indian is a sensation among the fun-loving and curious citizens, but unfortunately the Savage's reaction to the Brave New World is not as favorable. He refuses to take soma, is not impressed by the titillating entertainments, and retches violently at the sight of the great numbers of mindless and identical creatures. Disgusted and desperate, the Savage flees to a lonely lighthouse and seeks solitude and self-punishment, but he is hounded un-

16. Huxley, *Brave New World* (New York, 1932), p. 117.

mercifully—yet without malice—by curiosity seekers and "feelie" makers and is finally driven to suicide.

In the last scene of the novel, the Savage's lifeless body hangs in the lighthouse and, turning slowly, sightlessly gazes on a world in which creativity, love, and God have been crushed by the weight of human happiness:

> Slowly, very slowly, like two unhurried compass needles, the feet turned towards the right; north, north-east, east, southeast, south, south-south-west; then paused, and, after a few seconds, turned as unhurriedly back towards the left. South-south-west, south, southeast, east. [p. 311]

In *Brave New World* the few true human beings who have managed to resist Progress are deviants from the majority of society. Bernard Marx, Helmholtz Watson, and the Savage are all oddities in a world where the average man can't stand to be alone, blushes at the word "mother," and goes through life reciting the slogans which are, in fact, his total being. It is clearly not possible to be human and part of the system at the same time, for the essence of man is seen by Huxley as creativity, free will, recovery of natural passion, and these are heresies which the Brave New World has suppressed. The only member of the establishment who has remained human is Mustapha Mond, the world-controller, who, with a thorough knowledge of society both before and after Ford, freely chooses to side with the state and helps mold it with a brilliant but perverse creativity.

Bernard Marx is an unusual characterization in Huxley, for he is not a typed and static figure. Gradually, Huxley induces a shift in the reader's attitude toward Marx, from a thorough sympathy at the beginning of the novel to a scornful disdain at the close. Marx appeals to the reader at first because he does not fit into the Brave New World, but Bernard himself would very much like to be part of his society—to have the most pneumatic women, to be admired by the other alphas and feared by the lower castes. Unfortunately, a mistake during his hatching has made him smaller than average, neurotic, and maladjusted. Marx's intellectualism, his professed scorn for the values of his society are motivated not by an insight into the meaning of truth and beauty but by a hasty reaction formation to his alienation from the Brave New World. He loses the reader's sympathy when he uses the Savage as a device to gain attention. From this moment on, he diminishes from heroic to comic proportions and is finally revealed as a coward, begging to be allowed to stay in London rather than be sent to an island of misfits.

Helmholtz Watson, Bernard's friend, is a much more sympathetic character but remains a minor figure. If developed further, Watson could have been the successful alternative to the irreconcilable Savage and Mustapha Mond, as the person who finds meaning in creativity and poetry. But Watson is apparently introduced into the novel only to point out the decline of art into "emotional engineering" and the impossibility of free expression in the Brave New World.

Lenina Crowne, a pneumatic alpha whom the Savage at first adores as a goddess and a symbol of ultimate beauty, is generally a comic figure but with some tragic overtones. The reader senses that the ability to experience passion lies dormant within Lenina, but she has been trained to experience only mechanical, "rational" responses and does not have the imagination to transcend them. To the Savage's poetic ardors she can only respond with the words of a popular song, "Hug me till you drug me, honey."

Brave New World is a remarkable novel and, in many respects, the culmination of Huxley's art. The gruesome utopian vision, presented in marvelous detail and with awesome imaginativeness, holds the reader in horrified fascination. Huxley has escaped from his self-conscious pedantry, his uncertainty, his lapses in style, and writes with boldness and assurance. *Crome Yellow* and *Antic Hay* had been seriously marred by a lack of dramatic tension, but *Brave New World* manages to achieve such tension through the direct confrontation of equally powerful, conflicting philosophies. Unlike the earlier novels, there is a very real debate in *Brave New World,* and, interestingly enough, the outcome of the debate as presented within the novel is a grim stalemate.

Near the end of the novel, the Savage and the World-

Controller, Mustapha Mond, have a crucial argument. Mond
was a brilliant theoretical physicist with a knowledge of the
Bible, literature, and philosophy; but given a choice to be
sent to an island where he could continue his research or to
be taken on to the Controllers' Council, he chose the latter
and abandons the research. On the assumption that the
happiness and stability of man are the only ultimate ends,
all troubling qualities which upset men such as truth, beauty,
love, knowledge, pure science *are* dangers and must be suppressed. "God isn't compatible with machinery and scientific
medicine and universal happiness," Mond argues. The poetic
Savage, who mortifies his flesh and worships a stern and
terrible God, does not view this happiness and contentment
as man's end. "What you need," he says to the World-Controller, "is something with tears for a change. Nothing costs
enough here." Mustapha Mond astutely observes that the
Savage is "claiming the right to be unhappy." When the
Savage agrees defiantly, Mond goes on:

> "Not to mention the right to grow old and ugly and
> impotent; the right to have syphilis and cancer; the right
> to be lousy; the right to live in constant apprehension
> of what may happen to-morrow; the right to catch ty-
> phoid; the right to be tortured by unspeakable pains of
> every kind."
> There was a long silence.
> "I claim them all," said the Savage at last.
> Mustapha Mond shrugged his shoulders, "You're wel-
> come," he said.   [*Brave New World,* p. 288]

Who has won the argument? Both men on their own terms,
and neither; for Huxley and the reader, caught in between
the conflicting claims of "passion and reason, self-division's
cause," are locked in an irresolvable conflict, an unbreakable
stasis. Huxley is able to offer no solution, no reconciliation,
no alternative. D. H. Lawrence's notion of Noble Savagery,
which Huxley had flirted with, and even the fusion with
nature he had claimed as man's ideal, must be rejected in
the terms of *Brave New World.* Caught in the basic conflict
of the novel, they are torn apart and discredited. Half of the

creed resides with the closeness to nature and the savagery of the Indian reservation but inextricably is mingled there with disease, guilt, masochism, the hostile God. The other half is found in the sexual release and rejection of abstractions of the Brave New World, but is likewise sullied by the total dehumanization and absence of communication of its inhabitants. *Brave New World* is the darkest point and final stage of Huxley's pessimism. He is torn by irreconcilable views of man, and, admittedly, offers the reader the unenviable choice between "insanity on the one hand and lunacy on the other."[17]

With *Brave New World,* Huxley ends the first and most productive period of his life. It is obvious, at the close of this novel, that the spiritual crisis in Huxley had reached its greatest intensity and could go no further. Sadly enough, the author could find no earthly solution. Rejecting this world entirely in bitterness and disgust, Huxley adopted the philosophy of nonattachment, a mystical belief of Buddhist origins, which leads man away from the ugliness of bodily existence and immerses him in eternal, changeless verities. Huxley did not cease writing satirical novels, but even the best of his later satires, *After Many a Summer Dies the Swan,* is marred by the spirit of a man who hates life and is sinning against it. The subtle irony, the surprise of a beautiful passage, the delicate portrayal of character have disappeared and are replaced by a ruthless and brutal hatred.

Huxley's dilemma was a conflict between a skeptical, sophisticated mind and essentially Victorian morals. His scientific outlook, the First World War, the disillusionment of the '20s—these destroyed intellectually the validity of all but relative moral standards, but emotionally, he was in desperate need of absolutes. It was as if the spirits of his two famous ancestors, T. H. Huxley and Matthew Arnold, were locked in a mortal embrace in Huxley's soul. Huxley's tragedy is that of a man caught between two worlds, each with its own particular demands, truths, and horrors. Who can blame him for abandoning the struggle?

17. Huxley in the foreword to *Brave New World* (New York, Harper, 1960), p. xviii.

4 CONCLUSION

Evelyn Waugh, George Orwell, and Aldous Huxley were all, as satirists, examining life in the British Empire from the end of the First World War to the start of the present "Cold War," but they differ strikingly in style and judgment. Here are three sensitive, intelligent writers who have witnessed the same historical developments, lived through the same national and international crises, been influenced by the same culture, grown up in the same society, and yet their works reflect a remarkable diversity of interest, prejudice, and temperament. Evelyn Waugh, who supported Franco in the Spanish Civil War and who has been accused of flirting with Fascism, depicts the defeat of civilization by the forces of savagery, stupidity, and liberalism. George Orwell, who fought in the Spanish Republican Army against Franco and who proclaimed himself a revolutionary socialist, warns of the corrupting force of power and the evil spread of tyranny. Aldous Huxley, who was not terribly interested in political problems and who described himself as a type of mystic, portrays the progressive alienation of man and nature and attacks the growth of hedonism. The satirists are united in their conviction that there is something dreadfully wrong with society, but their peculiar visions of the sources of man's folly and evil differ radically.

Their differences in style and tone, too, seem to reflect entirely dissimilar world-views. Evelyn Waugh's novels are sophisticated, marvelously humorous, immensely polished fantasies depicting the giddy life of the Mayfair set, of the Bright Young People and their wealthy, imbecilic parents. Waugh's work is characterized further by the author's verbal brilliance, audacity, and almost complete detachment from his creations. Orwell's novels, on the other hand, are brooding, bitter, and explosive, portraying the filthy and cruel life beneath the thin veneer of bourgeois civilization. A work by Orwell is usually heavy with the author's physical disgust, passionate indignation, and deep personal involvement in his characters. Finally, Huxley's novels are intellectual, witty, and urbane, examining the life and opinions of a small group of young, well-educated, artistic sophisticates. Huxley, like Evelyn Waugh, maintains a careful detachment from his work, but his concern for the conflict of ideas and the "cozy little metaphysical shelters" of his characters is totally unlike Waugh.

The writing of satire, then, makes almost no demands for a particular belief or style. Waugh as a hardheaded conservative, Orwell as a revolutionary reformer, and Huxley as a mystic have contrary conceptions of evil and radically different methods of presenting their beliefs. And yet, throughout our reading of their novels, we are always aware that they are all satirists, that they are united in the writing of a special and unique kind of fiction. Waugh, Orwell, and Huxley, *because* of their great differences, are an ideal group from which to extract a notion of what satire is, to isolate and describe the essential characteristics of their particular form of literary expression.

These three are, of course, joined in the profound dislike of something in man and society and in the enterprise of attacking that which they dislike. But, while satire cannot exist without an object of attack, that attack itself does not necessarily constitute satire is evident from Cicero's bitter denunciations of Catiline or Hobbes' vicious description of the Catholic Church. An initial clue to the nature of satire may be seen in the difference, discussed earlier, between Cyril Connolly's critical analysis of the English preparatory school in *Enemies of Promise* and George Orwell's brilliant, satiric portrait of Crossgates in "Such, Such Were the Joys . . ." Both authors, we recall, attended the same school and reached similar conclusions about its faults, but Orwell went far beyond Connolly's bland didacticism by re-creating the suffering child's own vision of Crossgates. Orwell's essay, though written in the realistic mode, has an element of fantasy which is totally absent in Connolly's work and without which "Such, Such Were the Joys . . ." would not be satire. Similarly, Huxley's excellent nonsatirical essays criticize many of the ideas which are attacked in his satires, but in the satires the ideas are presented, even embodied, by fictional characters in a fictional context. Likewise, Evelyn Waugh's fine travel books and journalistic reports, like *Remote People* (1931) and *Waugh in Abyssinia* (1936), are written with the characteristic wit, mockery, and sophistication but lack the essential satirical fantasy of *Black Mischief* or *A Handful of Dust.*

The notion of fantasy as fundamental to satire by no means involves or implies an elaborate plot structure. Indeed, as Alvin Kernan points out in *The Cankered Muse,* "the most striking quality of satire is the absence of plot."[1] There is much action and noise in the novels we have examined, but rarely any significant change from the original settings of the works, never any meaningful and lasting achievements. In Waugh's *Decline and Fall,* Paul Pennyfeather is suddenly thrust out of his sheltered, scholarly existence into the mad, grotesque world of Margot Beste-Chetwynde, Alastair Digby-Vaine-Trumpington, and Augustus Fagan. Pennyfeather teaches at an insane school, becomes engaged to a beautiful socialite, is involved in a vice ring, is arrested and imprisoned minutes before his wedding, and is finally spirited from prison and pronounced dead. In spite of all these wild and outrageous events, however, the world at the close of the novel is precisely the world portrayed at the beginning—Paul returns to his quiet, sheltered existence, Margot to her vice ring, Alastair to his drunken orgies, Fagan to his fraud. The same pattern is repeated in the novels of Orwell and Huxley. The beasts in *Animal Farm* revolt against their piggish masters, attempt to alter their miserable condition, and are left, in the end, with equally and more obviously piggish masters. The characters in *Crome Yellow* paint, write, make love, and talk endlessly, seeking diversion or meaning in their lives, but they find neither.

In certain of the satirical novels we have studied, of course, there is a greater sense of movement and of plot: Tony Last, in *A Handful of Dust,* leaves Hetton Abbey, and embarks on an expedition to Brazil; Winston Smith, in *1984,* contacts the revolutionary underground; Gumbril, in *Antic Hay,* sets out to promote his patented pneumatic underclothes. The ap-

---

1. Kernan, *The Cankered Muse* (New Haven, 1959), p. 30.

parent movement, however, is only toward an intensifica-
tion of the ugliness and depravity that is present in the
satirical world from the beginning. Instead of a circle of
futility in these novels, there is a demonic spiral leading
downward through levels of increasing filth, despair, evil,
meaninglessness. Tony Last wanders in a steaming jungle
that is merely the ironic realization of his tangled and savage
domestic life; Winston Smith has contacted not a revolutionary but a leader in the Thought Police; Theodore Gumbril,
B.A. Oxon, has found the only cause to which he can wholly
devote himself, the promotion of comfortable underclothes.

The absence of a developing plot in satire is closely related
to the absence of developing characters. There is no expan-
sion of understanding, not only within the minor figures who
are all mindless caricatures, but within the major characters
as well. As we have seen in Chapter 1, complex and extensive
character study would be inconsistent with the satirist's attempt to show man's ugliness, pettiness, and mindlessness.
The characters of satire suffer but never transcend or even
comprehend their suffering, talk but never understand the
meaning of the words they speak, rebel but never know precisely what they are rebelling against. Adam Fenwick-Symes
and Nina Blount, in *Vile Bodies,* are lovers without the least
notion of the nature of love; John Flory, in *Burmese Days*
shoots himself in what might have been a heroic act but,
because of his shallowness, is only a final demonstration of
corrosive self-pity; Denis Stone, on his departure from Crome
Manor, is the same confused, callow, and childishly infatu-
ated young man he was on his arrival. The satirist never
allows his characters to rise to the level of true heroism or
true humanity, but always inflicts them with impotence,
keeping them the dupes or instruments of forces they cannot
control. In the novels of Evelyn Waugh the characters are
often mere mindless actors in a social drama; in Orwell, mere
symbols of overpowering political and social forces; in Huxley, mere embodiments of ideas. All three satirists, moreover,
portray men as subject to uncontrollable and often disgusting physical impulses and needs. The characters of satire are

not only unheroic—they are not even able to control their own bodily functions.

The weakness and passivity of the characters is essential to the single major theme that runs consistently throughout the works of all three satirists whom we have studied in this paper: the loss of human identity. In Waugh's novels man is dehumanized by becoming either an automaton or a savage. Professor Silenus, mechanically chewing a biscuit and pondering a world without men, and Basil Seal, eating his girl friend at a cannibal banquet, have suffered essentially the same fate, for they have both lost their reason, their sense of decency and civilization, their humanity. The Bright Young People in *Vile Bodies* are whirled like lifeless objects around an endless circle of parties and affairs, and, in Waugh's most despairing vision, Tony Last is forced by a madman to read again and again, like a machine, the collected works of Charles Dickens.

In the world of George Orwell, humans lose their individuality and identity by choosing to play a social role, as Elizabeth in *Burmese Days* chooses to be a burra memsahib or as Gordon Comstock in *Keep the Aspidistra Flying* finally surrenders to the aspidistra and to the loathsome bourgeois values the plant represents. In his later novels, particularly *1984,* Orwell pictures dehumanization in a much more comprehensive, systematized form, for he sees the total destruction of the human will and consciousness as both the foundation and the final goal of the modern state. Society is divided into rigid classes which destroy individual identity, and, at the same time, all men from all classes merge into the single, eternal consciousness of Big Brother, who is a collective being and not a human individual. O'Brien, one of the high priests of power in the monolithic state, describes the essence of politics to his helpless victim: "If you want a picture of the future, imagine a boot stamping on a human face—forever."[2]

Finally, Aldous Huxley sees man losing his human identity through the tyranny of ideas: "People who can reel off neatly formulated notions aren't quite real; they're slightly mon-

2. Orwell, *1984,* p. 271.

strous."[3] The characters of Huxley's early novels like *Crome Yellow* and *Antic Hay* seem intellectual and artistic, but they are actually devoid of intellect and imagination, for their ideas are their total being. True creativity must involve the whole man—the man of emotions as well as of intellect—and Huxley's sophisticates have willfully deadened their emotional sensitivity and broken their contact with nature. Like Orwell, Huxley came to see dehumanization as a sweeping, universal force. In *Brave New World*, however, man is crushed not by terror and brutality but by the overwhelming weight of conformity and the simple satisfaction of all desire. Huxley's ultimate vision of the destructions of the individual by progress and technology is the "Bokanovsky Group," the identical males and females created by the state, described here in a factory, merging with the equipment around them:

> The two low work-tables faced one another; between them crawled the conveyor with its load of separate parts; forty-seven blonde heads were confronted by forty-seven brown ones. Forty-seven snubs by forty-seven hooks; forty-seven receding by forty-seven prognathous chins. The completed mechanisms were inspected by eighteen identical curly auburn girls in Gamma green, packed in crates by thirty-four short-legged, left-handed male Delta-Minuses, and loaded into the waiting trucks and lorries by sixty-three blue-eyed, flaxen and freckled Epsilon Semi-Morons.[4]

In the midst of this world of relentless and cruel dehumanization stands the satiric "hero," the main character who has retained a small measure of individuality and aloofness, by being either a stranger (foreigner, savage, outsider) or a misfit in the depraved society. In the course of the satire the hero is exposed to the corrupting forces of meanness, imbecility, conformity, and greed and is affected in one of three ways: surrender, death, or a hopeless and unheroic continuation of the feeble resistance against both. In *Decline and Fall* Paul Pennyfeather is the naïve stranger, thrown into totally

3. Huxley, *Point Counter Point*, p. 307.
4. Huxley, *Brave New World*, p. 190.

unfamiliar surroundings and, though caught up in society, always alien to it. As a drunken friend tells Paul at the end of his adventures, "I think it was a mistake you ever got mixed up with us; don't you? We're different somehow."[5] Paul's escape from society is not a victory for individuality or humanity, however, but a sort of death to this world, as the mock death arranged by Margot and Fagan slyly testifies. Adam Fenwick-Symes in *Vile Bodies,* Basil Seal in *Black Mischief,* and Tony Last in *A Handful of Dust* are misfits, never comfortable or contented in their savage world, but never able to escape from it. Tony, who makes the most sustained attempt to live in his own private world, suffers the cruelest fate—death-in-life.

Orwell's heroes are more revolutionary than Waugh's, but their fate is the same. John Flory, in *Burmese Days,* violently (and impotently) attacks the corrupt system in which he is trapped but can only release himself by suicide. Gordon Comstock, in *Keep the Aspidistra Flying,* sinks into poverty in his revolt against bourgeois values but finally surrenders entirely to the money code. Winston Smith, in *1984,* feebly resists the tyrannical state but is taught the sinfulness of his rebellion and is left loving Big Brother and crying gin-scented tears of repentance.

Aldous Huxley's heroes fare no better. Denis Stone, in *Crome Yellow,* arrives at Crome Manor aware of his alienation from nature and the burden of his "twenty tons of ratiocination," but he cannot alter his unhappy state and returns to London even more disillusioned than before. Theodore Gumbril, in *Antic Hay,* is an unhappy misfit who almost finds meaningful love with Emily, but he surrenders to a whim of the temptress Myra Viveash and abandons all hope for the improvement of his condition. Finally, the Savage in *Brave New World,* is, of course, a stranger in a strange land who is only relieved from torture, disgust, and misery by suicide.

The satiric hero, then, suffers much and accomplishes nothing. His struggle takes no direction, leads to no increase

5. Waugh, *Decline and Fall* (London, 1928), pp. 237–38.

of knowledge or understanding, and never transcends his suffering or passes on to a comprehension of his fate. The absurdity of the character's agony and his inability to act or to understand radically diminishes the normal sympathy of the reader for the downtrodden and oppressed. Furthermore, in spite of the hero's hysterical insistence that he is innocent of all complicity in his fate, the reader senses that the hero's suffering is as much self-inflicted as generated by an alien and hostile society. Tony Last is such a fool that his destiny is not tragic but, in a perverse and bitterly ironic way, actually just and fitting. Gordon Comstock, with his tantrums, insolence, and self-pity is profoundly irritating in spite of his individuality. The Savage is noble, but he is also primitive, dirty, superstitious, and ignorant. In short, the satirist never allows his characters to engage too deeply the reader's sympathies, for the major subject of satire is not the nature of human suffering but the nature of human dullness.

In addition to the important formal and thematic qualities which, as we have seen, the satires of Evelyn Waugh, George Orwell, and Aldous Huxley have in common, there is striking similarity in the kind of imagery that is used to depict the evil in the universe. Again and again the reader confronts the same configurations of horror and depravity, which Northrop Frye, in the *Anatomy of Criticism,* describes as "demonic imagery":

> the world of the nightmare and the scapegoat, of bondage and pain and confusion; the world as it is before the human imagination begins to work on it and before any image of human desire, such as the city or the garden, has been solidly established; the world also of perverted or wasted work, ruins and catacombs, instruments of torture and monuments of folly.[6]

Frye proceeds to list the recurrent demonic symbols in the literature of the fallen universe. The political world is governed by the "tyrant-leader, inscrutable, ruthless, melancholy, and with an insatiable will" (p. 148), and is darkened

6. Frye, *Anatomy of Criticism,* p. 147.

by savagery and cannibalism. The demonic erotic relation is "a fierce destructive passion" (p. 149), and the social arrangement is the mob. The animal world is portrayed in terms of wild animals, monsters, or beasts of prey. The vegetable world is a sinister forest, a heath, a wilderness, or a sinister enchanted garden (and, presumably, a jungle) and may include such marginally "vegetable" images as the cross, the tree of death or forbidden knowledge, the stake, "scaffolds, gallows, stocks, pillories, whips, and birch rods" (p. 149). The inorganic world may remain in its "unworked form of deserts, rocks, and waste land," but is often portrayed in terms of "cities of destruction and dreadful night . . . , the great ruins of pride," prisons, catacombs, dungeons, and furnaces. Images of perverted work belong here too: "engines of torture, weapons of war, armor, and images of a dead mechanism which, because it does not humanize nature, is unnatural as well as inhuman" (p. 150).

It would be possible to track down and list the numerous particular variations of practically every one of these major symbols in the satires we have examined in this paper, but I do not feel that the space and effort required for such a task is justified, for the manifestations of this imagery in the novels of Waugh, Orwell, and Huxley should be at once evident. For Waugh, one thinks of Blackstone Gaol and the crazed "Lion of the Lord's elect" in *Decline and Fall;* the many unnatural deaths and the demonic nightmare of Agatha Runcible in *Vile Bodies;* the savagery and cannibalism in the jungle in *Black Mischief;* Tony Last's nightmares, the mindless cruelty of nature, the jungle with its figurative and real "ravening tigers," Tony as scapegoat, and the caged foxes in *A Handful of Dust.* For Orwell, one thinks of the incredible filth and inhumanity at Crossgates School; the tangled jungles, rat-infested cemeteries, ruined temples, and wasted lives in *Burmese Days;* Gordon Comstock's fantasies of war, his attempt to sink "down into the safe, soft womb of earth,"[7] the dreary slums in *Keep the Aspidistra Flying;* the cruel purges and the destroyed windmill in *Animal Farm;*

7. Orwell, *Keep the Aspidistra Flying*, p. 203.

and, of course, the elaborate perversion of religion, the torture, the rotting city, Winston Smith as scapegoat, the prisons, and Big Brother himself in *1984*. Orwell's two supposedly realistic reports—*Down and Out in Paris and London* and *The Road to Wigan Pier*—are also, as we have seen earlier, pervaded with demonic imagery, from the red-lit cellars of sin and filthy, stifling kitchens of the Parisian slums to the total devastation and emptiness of the slag heaps in the Welsh coal districts. For Huxley, one thinks of the revulsion for man's animal functions and the dwarfs and giants of *Crome Yellow;* the destructive eroticism of Myra Viveash, Coleman's diabolism, the monster in the night-club act, and the weird laboratory of the scientist in *Antic Hay;* the vast American Desert, the worship of the machine, the mindless Bokanovsky Groups, and the Savage's self-flagellation and suicide in *Brave New World.*

Frye, in his discussion of the demonic symbolism of the inorganic world, includes an image that I have chosen to reserve for a more general discussion: "Here too are the sinister counterparts of geometrical images: the sinister spiral (the maelstrom, whirlpool, or Charybdis), the sinister cross, and the sinister circle, the wheel fate or fortune" (p. 150). This demonic spiral or circle, which finds its greatest expression in Dante's *Inferno,* is, I think, central to practically every satire, for it is the form on which are disposed the details of each work. We have already seen the circle in the form of satire—the circular plots which start and end at approximately the same point. Thus the action of *Decline and Fall* moves from the Bollinger Club banquet at Scone College through the wild escapades of the central part of the novel and back, in the end, to the Bollinger Club banquet at Scone College a few years later. Similarly, at the opening of *Animal Farm* the animals are oppressed by their hoglike masters, and at the close, after their revolution has "succeeded," they are oppressed by the tyranny of the pigs. Finally, young, disillusioned Denis Stone arrives at Crome Manor from London at the beginning of *Crome Yellow* and departs for London equally disillusioned at the end.

The relation of this formal circle to the thematic circle is

evident, for satire concerns itself with the endless, meaningless cycles of existence, with futility and hopelessness, with
the inability to act, with the sinister wheel of fortune. The
characters are caught up in various social circles (for example, the endless round of parties in *Vile Bodies*) and are
dehumanized in their inability to exercise their will and
break out of the circles. The demonic spiral is also important
thematically, for the characters of satire are often drawn
deeper and deeper into the inferno that man creates on earth.

The importance of the circle and spiral is most clearly
seen, however, in the numerous images of demonic geometrical forms throughout the novels we have read. In *Decline and Fall* Professor Silenus states that life is "like the
big wheel at Luna Park":

> You pay five francs and go into a room with tiers of seats
> all around, and in the centre the floor is made of a great
> disc of polished wood that revolves quickly. At first you
> sit down and watch the others. They are all trying to
> sit in the wheel, and they keep getting flung off. . . . You
> see, the nearer you can get to the hub of the wheel the
> slower it is moving and the easier it is to stay on. . . . Of
> course, at the very centre there's a point completely at
> rest. . . . And when we do get to the middle, it's just as
> if we never started. It's so odd. [pp. 409–10]

This vision of the mechanical circle of futile death-in-life is
explored further in *Vile Bodies* in the nightmare of the dying
Agatha Runcible: "I thought we were driving round and
round in a motor race and none of us could stop." The
mechanical round of meaningless existence has its counter-
part in the savage dance in *Black Mischief* (a chain of sweating, frenzied bodies around the funeral pyre) and the bizarre
fate of Tony Last in *A Handful of Dust* (forced by a madman
in the jungle to read again and again the novels of Dickens).

In the novels of George Orwell the imagery of demonic
circles and spirals is rarely seen in the "pure" state in which
it is found in Waugh, but it is present in modified or suppressed images. In *Burmese Days*, for example, there is a
subtle image of the fate of the novel's hero and of the satirist

in general when John Flory, no longer able to stand the howling of a pariah dog, takes his rifle and fires at the animal:

> There was an echoing roar, and the bullet buried itself in the maiden, wide of the mark. A mulberry-coloured bruise sprang out on Flory's shoulder. The dog gave a yell of fright, took to its heels, and then, sitting down fifty yards farther away, once more began rhythmically baying. [p. 73]

Throughout the novel this circular pattern is repeated—Flory, losing control of himself, attacks the human beasts around him and only succeeds in bruising himself, while the dogs continue to howl obscenely. The circle of futility is succeeded in *Down and Out in Paris and London* by the description of the gangs of tramps "tens of thousands in number . . . marching up and down England like so many wandering Jews."[8] and in *The Road to Wigan Pier* by the image of the miner, trapped in his dismal, demoralizing, futile life.

Finally, the demonic circle is seen clearly in Huxley's satires, where, again, it is a symbol of wasted and empty lives. In *Antic Hay* science is satirized by the image of the physiologist Shearwater in his experimental hot-box, pedaling madly to turn the wheels of his stationary bicycle. The same novel ends with the great circular taxi ride taken by Gumbril and Mrs. Viveash round and round the dirty city of London. At the close of *Brave New World* the mindless sightseers who have come to gape at the Savage mortifying his flesh begin to mime the frenzy of the Savage's gestures and join together in an orgy of atonement:

> Then suddenly somebody started singing "Orgy-porgy" and, in a moment, they had all caught up the refrain and, singing, had begun to dance. Orgy-porgy, round and round and round, beating one another in six-eight time. Orgy-porgy . . .[9]

The mad dance of the inhabitants of the ultra-modern Brave New World brings us back to the frenzied savages

8. Orwell, *Down and Out in Paris and London*, p. 145.
9. Huxley, *Brave New World*, p. 310.

linked in a human chain in *Black Mischief* and the marching tramps of *Down and Out in Paris and London,* an indication of the unity of all satire. Waugh, Orwell, and Huxley, in spite of their different backgrounds and attitudes, all see men as caught up in a horrid circle of dehumanization, futility, madness, evil. In creating images of this demonic circle, in writing satire, they relieve the unbearable pressure of anger and dismay in their breasts and, at the same time, express a coherent and relatively stable artistic world-view. Furthermore, it may be that by heightening our awareness of the demonic circles in which we ourselves are trapped, the satirist gives us the power to break out of those circles and to recover a life with true direction, meaning, and humanity.

WORKS CITED

Atkins, John, *Aldous Huxley*, New York, 1956.

Bergson, Henri, "Laughter," in *Comedy*, ed. Wylie Sypher, Garden City, New York, 1956.

Brander, Laurence, *George Orwell*, London, 1954.

Brewster, Dorothy, and Angus Burrel, *Modern Fiction*, New York, 1934.

· Brooke, Jocelyn, *Aldous Huxley*, London, 1954.

Burgum, Edwin B., *The Novel and the World's Dilemma*, New York, 1947.

Connolly, Cyril, *Enemies of Promise*, London, 1938.

DeVitis, A. A., *Roman Holiday: The Catholic Novels of Evelyn Waugh*, New York, 1956.

Dooley, David J., "The Limitations of George Orwell," *University of Toronto Quarterly*, 28 (1958–59), 291–99.

Edgar, Pelham, *The Art of the Novel*, New York, 1933.

Ellis, G. U., *Twilight on Parnassus*, London, 1939.

Frierson, William C., *The English Novel in Transition*, Norman, Oklahoma, 1942.

Frye, Northrop, *Anatomy of Criticism*, Princeton, 1957.

Gerber, Richard, *Utopian Fantasy*, London, 1955.

· Ghose, Sisirkumar, *Aldous Huxley*, New York, 1962.

Henderson, Philip, *The Novel Today*, London, 1936.

Hollis, Christopher, *George Orwell*, Chicago, 1956.

Hopkinson, Tom, *George Orwell*, London, 1953.

Hull, James, *The Growth of a Personality*, Zurich, 1955.

· Huxley, Aldous, *After Many a Summer Dies the Swan*, New York, 1939.

———, *Antic Hay*, New York, 1923.

———, *Ape and Essence*, New York, 1948.

———, *Brave New World*, New York, 1932.

———, *Collected Essays*, New York, 1960.

———, *Crome Yellow*, New York, 1922.

———, *Point Counter Point*, New York, 1928.

· ———, *World of Aldous Huxley*, ed. Charles J. Rolo, New York, 1947.

Karl, Frederick R., *The Contemporary English Novel*, New York, 1959.

Kernan, Alvin B., *The Cankered Muse*, New Haven, 1959.

———, "The Wall and the Jungle: The Early Novels of Evelyn Waugh," *Yale Review, 53* (1963), 199–220.

Leyburn, Ellen Douglass, "Animal Stories," in *Modern Satire,* ed. Alvin Kernan, New York, 1962.

· Linklater, Eric, *The Art of Adventure*, London, 1947.

MacCarthy, Desmond, *Criticism*, London, 1932.

Martin, Graham, "Novelists of Three Decades: Evelyn Waugh, Graham Greene, C. P. Snow," *The Modern Age*, Pelican Guide to English Literature, 7, Baltimore, 1961.

Maurois, André, *Poets and Prophets*, trans. Hamish Miles, London, 1936.

Newby, Philip H., *The Novel: 1945–1950*, London, 1951.

O'Faolain, Sean, *The Vanishing Hero*, London, 1956.

Orwell, George, *Animal Farm*, New York, 1946.

———, *Burmese Days*, New York, 1934.

———, *A Collection of Essays*, New York, 1954.

———, *Coming Up for Air,* New York, 1939.

———, *Down and Out in Paris and London*, New York, 1933.

———, *Homage to Catalonia*, London, 1938.

———, *Keep the Aspidistra Flying*, New York, 1936.

———, *1984*, New York, 1949.

———, *The Road to Wigan Pier*, London, 1937.

Rees, Richard, *George Orwell: Fugitive from the Camp of Victory*, Carbondale, 1961.

Rosenfeld, Isaac, *An Age of Enormity*, Cleveland, 1943.

· Savage, D. S., "Aldous Huxley and the Dissociation of Personality," in *Critiques and Essays on Modern Fiction,* ed. J. W. Aldridge, New York, 1952.

Stopp, Frederick J., *Evelyn Waugh: Portrait of an Artist*, Boston, 1958.

Swinnerton, Frank, *The Georgian Literary Scene*, London, 1935.

Waugh, Evelyn, *Black Mischief*, London, 1932.

———, *Brideshead Revisited*, London, 1944.

———, *Decline and Fall*, London, 1928.

———, *A Handful of Dust,* London, 1934.

———, *The Loved One,* London, 1948.

———, *Put Out More Flags*, London, 1942.

———, *Remote People*, London, 1931.

————, *Scoop,* London, 1937.

————, *Vile Bodies,* London, 1930.

————, *Waugh in Abyssinia,* London, 1936.

Wilson, Edmund, " 'Never Apologize, Never Explain': The Art of Evelyn Waugh," *Classics and Commercials,* New York, 1950.

INDEX